Torture

Torture

Does It Make Us Safer? Is It Ever OK?

A Human Rights Perspective

**EDITED BY KENNETH ROTH AND MINKY WORDEN
AMY D. BERNSTEIN, CONTRIBUTING EDITOR**

Published in Conjunction with Human Rights Watch

*2 aug. '06
For Richard—
Thanks for
caring and for
making a difference
with your
creative
vision.
Jane Olson*

THE NEW PRESS

NEW YORK
LONDON

HUMAN
RIGHTS
WATCH

Published in the United States by The New Press, New York, 2005
Distributed by W. W. Norton & Company, Inc., New York

"Respecting the Geneva Conventions" by John McCain (originally published as
"In Praise of Do-Gooders") reprinted from The Wall Street Journal
© 2004 Dow Jones & Company. All rights reserved.

LIBRARY OF CONGRESS CATALOGING-IN-PUBLICATION DATA

Torture : does it make us safer? is it ever ok?
a human rights perspective / edited by Kenneth Roth and Minky Worden.
p.   cm.
"Published in conjunction with Human Rights Watch."
Includes bibliographical references.
ISBN 1-56584-971-X
1. Torture.   2. Human rights.   I. Roth, Kenneth.   II. Worden, Minky.
III. Human Rights Watch (Organization)
HV8593.T6623   2005
179.7—dc22   2005047966

The New Press was established in 1990 as a not-for-profit alternative to the large,
commercial publishing houses currently dominating the book publishing industry.
The New Press operates in the public interest rather than for private gain, and is committed
to publishing, in innovative ways, works of educational, cultural, and community value
that are often deemed insufficiently profitable.

www.thenewpress.com

Composition by dix!
This book was set in Bembo

Printed in the United States of America

2   4   6   8   10   9   7   5   3   1

To Bob Bernstein
for the inspiration
behind this book and his
decades fighting
torture worldwide.

"From the depths of my cell, from the depths of madness, I took an oath that if I got out alive, I would fight for justice for all the victims of torture, particularly those who died in my arms. I am convinced that God allowed me to remain alive in order to carry out this mission, in memory of those who died and disappeared. And most of all, to prevent this from ever happening again."

—Souleymane Guengueng, who nearly died of mistreatment in
the prisons of Chadian dictator Hissène Habré (1982–1990). He
collected evidence of hundreds of cases of torture and killings and
is working with Human Rights Watch to bring Habré to justice.

Contents

PART II: TORTURE AND THE UNITED STATES

Introduction

Kenneth Roth

Who would have thought it still necessary to debate the merits of torture? Sure, governments have always tortured, but usually they did it clandestinely. Historically, torture has been seen as inherently shameful—something that, when practiced, was done in the shadows. International law had no prohibition more basic than the ban on torture. Even the right to life admitted exceptions—such as the killing of combatants allowed in wartime—but torture was forbidden unconditionally, whether in time of peace or war, whether at the local police precinct or in the face of a major security threat.

Yet, suddenly, following the terrorist attacks of September 11, 2001, torture and related mistreatment have become serious policy options for the United States. Once the leading governmental defender of human rights around the world, the U.S. government has now become the most influential abuser. American academics are proposing ways to regulate the pain that can be inflicted on suspects in detention. Overly clever U.S. government lawyers have tried to define away laws against torture. The Bush Administration claims latitude to abuse detainees that its predecessors would never have dared.

To their great surprise, many Americans thus find themselves looking for guidance on the fundamental issues surrounding torture. What constitutes torture? Does it ever work? Is it ever morally acceptable? These questions have acquired a new urgency for Americans and, by extension, for the world.

This book was assembled in an effort to supply some answers. We looked to those with expertise about the issues surrounding torture—whether derived through firsthand monitoring of torturing countries, such as Sir Nigel Rodley acquired in his capacity as UN Special Rapporteur on Torture, or through personal victimization by a torturous regime, such as endured in Argentina by Juan Méndez and the father of Héctor Timerman. Our hope is to offer a context for thinking about America's current dilemma in an informed, nuanced way.

Most human rights activists, including those at Human Rights Watch, endorse an absolute ban on torture, any time, anywhere, as international law prescribes. Torture, in our view, dehumanizes people by treating them as pawns to be manipulated through their pain. It harnesses the awesome power of the state and applies it to human beings at their most vulnerable. Breaching any restraint of reciprocity, it subjects the victim to abuse the perpetrator would never himself want to suffer.

But should torture *always* be outlawed? James Ross describes the historical evolution of the torture ban. Eitan Felner examines Israel's experimentation with a supposedly limited exception to that ban, justified by invoking the classic "ticking bomb" scenario. Marie-Monique Robin looks at France's use of torture in its former colonies. And Michael Ignatieff considers the costs, in dangerous times, of *not* using torture.

The word "torture" has entered the vernacular to describe a host of irritants, but this book addresses exclusively "state-sponsored" torture in the context of international law, where the definition of torture is quite specific: the intentional infliction of severe pain or suffering, whether physical or mental, for whatever reason, when the perpetrators are not private actors but government officials or those operating with their consent or acquiescence.

Why do governments torture? Minky Worden illustrates in her survey of practices around the world today that governments torture for a variety of reasons. In Brazil, for example, criminal suspects are routinely tortured to extract confessions for everyday crimes. In Uzbekistan and Egypt, torture is used to eradicate political dissent and to meet perceived security threats. Some countries, such as China and, historically, Turkey, torture to silence critics. At the level of the individual torturer, sadism, revenge, and frustration can each play a role as well. And now, for the United States, torture and related forms of coercive interrogation have become tools for addressing the threat of terrorism.

Torture exists on a continuum of mistreatment. Abuse just short of torture is known in international law as cruel, inhuman, or degrading treatment. The line between these concepts is not well defined—lesser forms of mistreatment are often gateways to torture—which is one reason why international law prohibits all these forms of coercion. The danger of authorizing even limited coercion is illustrated by Reed Brody's chapter on "The Road to Abu Ghraib." The legal consequences of senior leaders crossing these lines is explored by Dinah Pokempner in her essay on command responsibility. Tom Malinowski looks at the effect of the Bush Administration's use of torture and mistreatment on America's diminished standing in the world.

Ultimately, as we hope this book helps to demonstrate, torture and related abuses under any circumstance are antithetical to the entire concept of human rights. Rights define the limits beyond which no government should venture. To breach those limits in the name of some utilitarian calculus is to come dangerously close to the ends-justify-the-means rationale of terrorism. By contrast, a society that rejects torture affirms the essential dignity and humanity of each individual. A society that refrains from torture is best able to find common ground with would-be allies around the world, building a cooperative front against terrorism and presenting a positive ideal that is the bane of terrorist recruiters. And a society that eschews torture upholds the rules of human rights that, in the end, provide the best argument for why it is wrong for the terrorist to attack ordinary civilians.

Torture

PART I

International Torture

1

A HISTORY OF TORTURE

James Ross

James Ross is Senior Legal Advisor at Human Rights Watch. He has written extensively on criminal justice and the use of torture in Southeast Asia, most notably Cambodia, Indonesia, and the Philippines. He has participated in human rights fact-finding missions to more than two dozen countries in Asia, Africa, and the Balkans. In this piece, Ross traces the torture debate through history.

In 1764, Pietro Verri, a Milanese aristocrat and intellectual, completed a scathing treatise on the practice of torture. But to publish it would have humiliated his father, a respected senator who had long opposed Austrian rule over Milan by defending traditional practices, including the use of torture to obtain confessions. So Verri, along with his brother Alessandro, a prison administrator, sought help from the Society of Fists, a reformist group whose name derived not from the punch it carried but from the fisticuffs that invariably ended meetings. They found it in a brilliant but indolent twenty-five-year-old marquis named Cesare Beccaria.

With Verri's prodding and editing, Beccaria wrote *On Crimes and Punishments.* In a few dozen pages, Beccaria denounced torture and other judicial practices of the day and drew a link between society's treatment of criminals and the prevention of crime. Torture, he wrote, "is a sure route for the acquittal of robust ruffians and the conviction of weak innocents." To Verri's everlasting consternation, Beccaria's little pamphlet became a bestseller throughout Europe—and eventually the most influential work on criminal justice ever written.

By century's end, most nations in Europe had banned judicial torture—that is, torture lawfully used to compel confessions and testimony. Historians have challenged whether Beccaria changed European thinking on torture or merely captured emerging judicial and humanitarian trends. Yet the result was to ensure that judicial torture, an accepted practice in Europe for more than five centuries, would thereafter bear the burden of moral opprobrium. While the reality of torture is very much with us today, it remains universally condemned. The attacks of September 11, 2001, and the campaign against global terrorism have, however, renewed the debate over torture's legitimacy.

This essay spans twenty-five hundred years of state-imposed torture in Europe: from ancient Greece and Rome, the resurrection of judicial torture in the late Middle Ages, the Inquisition and later witch hunts, to judicial torture's abolition in the eighteenth century and its return in the twentieth. It considers not *how* people were tortured but rather the justifications for and criticisms of its use. And it seeks to explain why the post–World War II human rights treaties, which banned torture absolutely, have failed to fully convince the public that even in an age of terror, torture is forever unacceptable.

Ancient Greece and Rome

In ancient Greece, slaves and foreigners could lawfully be tortured to provide confessions and eyewitness testimony in legal disputes, but free citizens were not subject to torture. The rationale was not simply a question of status but reflected society's vision of the obtainment of truth. The testimony of a free citizen was considered to be tainted by his capacity to reason, which could produce truth or lies. Thus, while breaking an oath by lying in court risked expulsion from society, a free citizen might still reason that the risk was worth taking.

Greek courts instead recognized a slave's testimony extracted by torture as the highest form of truth. Slaves were expected to lie if questioned openly, particularly if they feared punishment from their master. But if tortured, slaves were considered to have sufficient reason to tell the truth—to end the torture. Thus the Greek legal orator Demosthenes, among others, could argue:

> Wherever slaves and free men are present and facts have to be found, you [the jury] do not use the statements of the free witnesses, but you seek to discover the truth by applying torture [*basanos*] to the slaves. Quite properly, men of the jury, since witnesses have sometimes been found not to have given true evidence, whereas no statements made as a result of torture have ever been proved untrue.[1]

Those who questioned the use of torture included Aristotle, who notably addressed the issue in his instruction on the techniques of persuasion, *Rhetoric:* "Torture is a kind of evidence, which appears trustworthy, because a sort of compulsion is attached to it." But he pointed out that "those under compulsion are as likely to give false evidence as true, some being ready to endure everything rather than tell the truth, while others are really ready to make false charges against others, in the hope of being sooner released from torture."[2] But while Aristotle the pragmatist questioned evidence obtained through torture, he never contested the practice of torturing slaves.

The Roman republic followed the Greek practice in legal proceedings of subjecting only slaves to torture. With the expansion of Roman authority under the Empire, the neat distinction between free citizen and slave blurred, as there developed after the second century CE a class of freed slaves and non-Romans with partial rights of citizenship. During the late Empire, judicial torture was extended to include this very large group of second-class citizens.

The legal basis for torture in Rome could be found in Justinian's

Code, a collection of imperial constitutions, and *Digest,* the opinions of jurists. Chapter Eighteen of Book Forty-Eight of the *Digest,* "De Quaestionibus" ("On Torture"), would later provide classical authority for torture in the civil law systems of Europe. Roman legal writers endlessly debated the efficacy of torture. According to the famed jurist Ulpian:

> [T]orture is not always to be trusted, nor is it always to be disbelieved: it is a delicate, dangerous and deceptive thing. For many persons have such strength of body and soul that they heed pain very little, so that there is no means of obtaining the truth from them; while others are so susceptible to pain that they will tell any lie rather than suffer it.[3]

As the modern historian Edward Peters has written, "Instead of questioning the method, the [Romans] surrounded it with a jurisprudence that was designed to give greater assurance to its reliability, a jurisprudence that is admirable in its skepticism and unsettling in its logic."[4]

Crucially, there was one context in which free citizens of Greece and Rome could be subjected to torture: in cases of treason. Though never judicially permitted, rulers seemed to have few qualms about using their extrajudicial powers to torture those suspected of plotting against them. And while there were those who questioned the excesses of Rome's unstable caesars, the use of torture to protect the emperor was not seriously challenged.

For Roman authorities, it was not a major leap to extend the practice of torturing traitors (those rejecting the *corporeal* authority of the emperor) to torturing the new Christians (those rejecting the emperor's *heavenly* authority). The early church leader Tertullian exposed the unique nature of their cruel treatment: A suspected Christian would first be tortured to confess to the crime of being a Christian, then tortured again to denounce the faith the authorities had tried so hard to elicit. These justifications for torture, like the "De Quaestionibus," would also have long-term historical consequences.

The Civil Law Revolution

In the long period after Rome's fall—roughly from the sixth to the twelfth century—"criminal law" was predominately private, and public authorities did not actively investigate offenses. Instead, an injured person would bring accusations against the alleged perpetrator and find a court that had jurisdiction over both parties. If the swearing of freeman's oaths did not elicit the truth, the court would turn the matter over to the "judgment of God," that is, resort to trial by ordeal or judicial combat.

While such practices eventually came to be judged as primitive, barbaric, and irrational, they provided little opportunity for the authorities, whether secular or ecclesiastical, to engage in torture. Expressing sentiments that the Catholic Church would not repeat for nearly a thousand years, Pope Nicholas I in 866 castigated the use of torture in Bulgaria, which then was considering joining the Western church: "A confession must be spontaneous, not extracted by force. Will you not be ashamed if no proof emerges from the torture? Do you not recognize how iniquitous your procedure is?"[5]

The twelfth century witnessed a revolution in law.[6] Central was the emergence of public law, which required codified laws and a judicial system staffed with trained judges and state prosecutors. The new system sought to do away with the irrationalities of the accusatorial process. Officials in Italy and France looking for a source of authority latched onto Roman law, which legal scholars versed in the *Code* and the *Digest* accepted as an expression of supreme legal reasoning.

The civil-law justice system developed a rigid structure for the prosecution of serious offenses. Two elements, a perpetrator and circumstantial evidence of a crime, known as *indicia,* were necessary to bring forward a prosecution and justify the interrogation of the accused. But *indicia* alone were not enough for a conviction. Convictions required "proofs": the testimony of two eyewitnesses or the confession of the accused.

In this way, an effort to rationalize and reform the law instead brought about an acceptance of the torture chamber for five hundred years. It should be noted that the revival of judicial torture arose from the rules of evidence adopted, rather than from any genuine requirements of ancient Roman law. Finding the two eyewitnesses to convict frequently proved impossible, leaving confessions as the primary basis for convictions. The criminal confession, considered no less sacred than a sacramental confession, gained the status of the "queen of proofs." This provided easy encouragement for local magistrates, and later judges and prosecutors, to impose torture.

As torture flourished, so did rules to regulate it. Torture to obtain confessions was permitted so long as it matched the severity of the crime and the strength of the *indicia* against the accused. Rules detailed the manner in which torture could be conducted and the judicial officers who needed to be present (which did not include defense counsel). Later developments allowed for witnesses as well as defendants to be tortured. Thus, unlike Greek and Roman law, which permitted torture based on the status of the accused, the emerging justice systems of Europe integrated torture into general legal procedure.

Roman law procedure was rapidly adopted by states on the continent. The new technology of moveable type helped to disseminate and regularize legislation and jurisprudence throughout Europe. Numerous legal scholars sought to explain and improve upon the system. The fifteenth-century Flemish jurist Philippe Wielant justified torture as "a simple regard for truth and a demand for such perfect proof that nothing short of a confession would satisfy it." (He urged that a truthful confession could easily be assured by torturing a son in the presence of his father, and a wife before her husband.)[7]

The Dutch legal scholar Johannes Voet at the turn of the seventeenth century argued that torture was a natural method of obtaining evidence by which criminals would convict themselves. For him simply because torture was at times misused or abused did not invalidate its practice within the criminal justice system. Voet urged the development of comprehensive rules for torture's application. These rules permitted torture only when there were "grave presumptions" against the accused and required that torture not cause death; that the youngest or most timid of a group be tortured first (presumably to reduce the need to torture the more strong-willed); and that an accused who confessed under torture not be tortured again, unless he or she recanted.[8] Such arguments ultimately led states to develop official handbooks that provided minutely detailed instruction on torture.

Criticism of torture largely limited itself to its misapplication and only very rarely advocated its prohibition. While there were undoubtedly those who genuinely wanted to strengthen judicial safeguards over increasingly abusive practices, the effect was to further legitimize a system whose consequences—death, mutilation, and false convictions—were widely known. For instance, Joost Damhouder, in his 1554 advice to the "Good Judge," impressed upon judges their critical role in ensuring that torture stayed within legal bounds: "Take no notice of the screams, cries, sighs, tremblings or pain of the accused; and all must be done with such care and moderation that the patient be neither driven mad, wounded, hurt nor unduly distressed."[9] And the Dutch lawyer Antonius Matthaeus II in 1644 provided an ostensibly complete list of objections to the practice of torture, including: the affront to natural justice by torturing an innocent; the possibility that the accused person's perception of truth would be skewed under torture; and the impossibility of ever learning the truth of guilt or innocence should the accused die.[10] For Matthaeus and many others, the problem was not torture per se but the danger that it could be used against the innocent.

In summarizing some five hundred years of legally sanctioned torture, it is worth noting one of the few justice systems in Europe that rejected it. In England, the common law banned the use of torture to compel confessions.[11] Jury trials permitted convictions based solely on circumstantial evidence, eliminating the pressure of civil law's strict evidentiary requirements to obtain confessions. That said, torture was used by the Star Chamber, the notorious royal court established in 1487, originally to try persons accused of treason. The Star Chamber acted on the extraordinary power of the Crown and wholly outside the common-law court system. Over time it expanded its jurisdiction and its ill-treatment of those before it: torture became permissible for obtaining the names of accomplices as well as confessions. The Star Chamber's abuse of power, though not specifically its resort to torture, led to its abolition in the 1640s.

The Inquisition and Great Witch Hunts

A parallel practice of torture developed under canon law, most notably during the Roman Catholic Church's far-reaching campaign against heresy—the Inquisition. In 1252, Pope Innocent IV formally authorized the use of torture against heretics. Heresy, essentially "treason against God," was treated just like a serious crime before the civil courts, requiring two witnesses or a confession. Since heresy was almost always a crime of conscience, confessions and the threat or use of torture to obtain them was common. Not unlike Rome's persecution of the early Christians, the Inquisitors first tortured suspected heretics to make them confess to the crime, and then tortured them again to force them to renounce their beliefs.

The great witch hunts of Europe widened the practice of torture in both the Church and in the civil courts. The Papal Bull of Innocent VIII in 1484, and the *Malleus Maleficarum (Hammer of the Witches)* issued two years later, ushered in witch hunts throughout the continent that would claim from 200,000 to one million lives, mostly women, over the next two centuries. Witchcraft and sorcery had long been considered a civil crime subject to local retribution, but the imprimatur of the Church gave religious sanction to the persecution of suspected witches. Inquisitional methods of torture were applied to root out witches, and as the Inquisition faded into history, the civil courts took the lead in the witch hunts.

The need for denunciations rather than simple confessions was a central element of the witch hunts. Because witches were believed to take part in the "sabbat"—a nighttime assembly—it was not enough for the authorities to eliminate an individual witch; hunts required seeking out and destroying all the sect's members. Although witch hunts occurred sporadically and with some measure of isolation from one another, the practice of denunciation resulted in an exponential loss of life that could prove devastating in a particular locale. Frequently the torture and executions would stop only when the wives of the town councilors found themselves among those denounced.

Whereas any criticism of the Inquisition was likely to get one declared a heretic, it was possible to attack the use of torture in witchcraft cases. Virtually all who wrote on the subject accepted the reality of witches. The French jurist Jean Bodin in the late sixteenth century called for caution in the use of torture against witches—but only because witches had the power to render themselves impervious to pain—and urged torture to instead be used on "children and delicate persons." [12] Physician Johann Weyer, the most famous Protestant opponent of the witch hunts, was outspoken against torture:

> Those wretched women, whose minds have already been disturbed by the delusions and arts of the devil and are now upset by frequent torture, . . . and constantly dragged out to undergo atrocious torment until

they would gladly exchange at any moment this most bitter existence for death, are willing to confess whatever crimes are suggested to them rather than be thrust back into their hideous dungeon amid ever-recurring torture.[13]

Among the most forceful critics of the torture of accused witches was the Jesuit Friedrich von Spee, whose *Cautio Criminalis,* published in 1631, helped end the witch hunts in Germany. Spee invoked the general population's belief in witches to undercut the ill-treatment of those so accused: "It is assumed that a woman cannot endure two or three tortures unless she is a witch. . . . But this is to admit that the torture, as beyond human endurance, was excessive—and therefore illegal, and the accused [should] neither be tortured again nor condemned."[14]

Enlightenment and Reform

When Cesare Beccaria penned *On Crimes and Punishments* in 1764, the historical tide was already turning on torture. Enlightenment thinkers, such as Montesquieu and Voltaire, had emphasized the confluence of morality and rationality in which torture could play no part. As historian Malise Ruthven has written, "Beccaria was not a lone prophet crying in the wilderness. Many eighteenth-century writers considered it self-evident that torture was a horrible relic of barbarism, compounded of tyranny and superstition, and with the progress of reason and enlightenment destined to disappear from the face of the earth."[15]

Beccaria's arguments against torture were not novel. It was not so much what Beccaria said but the simple and direct language with which he said it. He considered torture to be both unjust and irrational. It was unjust because it betrayed the ideals of the social contract: "No man can be judged a criminal until he be found guilty; nor can society take from him the public protection, until it have been proved that he has violated the conditions on which it was granted." The irrationality of torture lay at the heart of Beccaria's denunciation. Should the suspect be guilty, he wrote, then "he should only suffer the punishment ordained by the laws, and torture becomes useless, as his confession is unnecessary. If he be not guilty, you torture the innocent; for in the eyes of the law, every man is innocent, whose crime has not been proved." Thus the guilty as well as the innocent must be spared from torture.

In the decades that followed, the great European legal codes had their detailed instructions on torture expunged. The revolutionaries in France might well have used the guillotine without qualms, but their victims were not tortured first. Changing practices in the criminal justice system certainly played a major part. Well before the appearance of *On Crimes and Punishments,* the civil-law rules of evidence had become less rigid. In the sixteenth and seventeenth centuries, incarceration and forced labor replaced execution and corporal punishment for many offenses, and discretionary sentences permitted judges greater use of circumstantial evidence. These developments weakened the demand on courts to obtain the formal full proof that had in practice perpetuated the use of torture. Taken altogether, Enlightenment morality and rationality, crucial changes in the law of evidence, and Beccaria's inspiring words brought about a widespread social movement that eliminated torture as a tool of criminal justice on the European continent.

The End of Torture—And Its Return

In 1874, Victor Hugo famously declared that "torture has ceased to exist." At least in Europe this was largely true, during wartime as well as peacetime. Prohibitions against the torture of prisoners of war were enshrined in treaties based upon the first modern codification of the laws of war, the Lieber Code, drafted in 1863 during the American Civil War. The Lieber Code banned torture under all circumstances: "Military necessity does not admit of cruelty—that is, the infliction of . . . torture to extort confessions." [16]

However, torture continued to be practiced along the fringes of the criminal justice system, both within the state and outside of it. Torture was used against those deemed a threat to the government, notably revolutionaries in Italy and Austria after the cataclysms of 1848, and against opponents of the Tsarist regime in Russia. In Europe's colonies, the legal and social movement against torture had little impact. The British, for instance, made only superficial efforts to stop torture in India. The Congo under Belgian domination relied on torture for its slave-driven economy. And as the history of the French in Algeria during the 1960s made clear, torture remained part of colonial rule up to independence, and fueled practices in newly independent states that have been hard to extinguish.

Still, torture as an acceptable element of criminal justice was dead, and remains dead. But torture in the name of state security, never fully abandoned, was to return in the twentieth century with a vengeance.

The political maneuvering in Europe in the decades before the First World War saw the proliferation of foreign spies, *agents provocateurs,* and terrorists. When caught, they were viewed as actors outside the existing legal order, subject to treatment otherwise prohibited by the regular rules of justice. And increasing demand for actionable intelligence on the battlefield since the First World War has rendered the absolute legal ban on torture of prisoners—in practice, but not in law—far less than absolute.

Torture for an ostensibly higher purpose became legacies of the radical states of the Left and the Right that arose in the 1920s and '30s. Soviet Russia, Fascist Italy, and later Nazi Germany exacted total obedience from their populations: the opponents of the state were the new traitors, the new heretics. These states reacted to any and all perceived internal threats with torture. Torture was inflicted not just to generate confessions and denunciations but to instill terror in the population. Stalin's purges of the Communist Party during the 1930s used torture to "uncover" ever-widening circles of counterrevolutionaries where no real counterrevolution existed. Torture in the name of state security became a hallmark of the Khmer Rouge in Cambodia in the 1970s; the regime's bureaucratic abominations included a forty-two-page interrogation manual for use at its Tuol Sleng torture center.

The horrors of the Second World War were realized in many ways, but the Nazi torture chambers in particular left their mark on the drafters of the human rights and humanitarian law treaties of the postwar period. The 1948 Universal Declaration of Human Rights adopted an absolute ban on torture without controversy and recognized what has been described as the drafters' intention: "to eliminate the medieval methods of torture and cruel punishment which were practiced in the recent past by the Nazis and fascists."[17] The Geneva Conventions of 1949 ban all use of "mutilation, cruel treatment and torture" of prisoners of war and detained civilians during all armed conflicts.[18] The 1966 International Covenant on Civil and Political Rights prohibits torture even "during public emergencies that threaten the life of the nation."[19] And the 1984 Convention against Torture and Other Cruel, Inhuman or Degrading Treatment or Punishment states unequivocally: "No exceptional circumstances whatsoever, whether a state of war or a threat of war, internal political instability or any other public emergency, may be invoked as a justification of torture."[20] The prohibition against torture was complete.

The human rights treaties can be viewed as the culmination of a historical process recognizing the inviolability of the person. Today no justice system formally permits torture and no government openly considers it acceptable. Yet day in and day out, far too many people throughout the world suffer under a torturer's hands. Police officers ignore local prohibitions to beat and break information out of criminal suspects. Judges convict on the basis of obviously coerced confessions. In many developing countries the lack of modern forensic tools makes torture an easy alternative to serious investigations. Police corruption and ineptitude are further factors. As Sir James Fitzjames Stephen observed in his 1883 analysis of the Madras Commission report on torture in colonial India, "It is far pleasanter to sit comfortably in the shade rubbing red pepper into a poor devil's eyes than to go about in the sun hunting up evidence."[21] Whether in Shanghai or Chicago, it seems police will be tempted to use the "third degree" whenever they can get away with it.

Today's dedicated opponents of torture rest their case on the absolute prohibition found in international human rights law. But the popular moral outrage that for two centuries has rejected judicial torture is not so deeply embedded for torture carried out under the guise of state security. The September 11 attacks on the United States and the resulting "war on terrorism" have resurrected the previously unthinkable topic of the legitimacy of state torture. Interestingly, none of the officials or academics who have argued for the controlled application of torture have suggested that the information gained be admissible in court. In their view it is about security, not prosecutions. Although the powers sought for state security are in no way comparable to those of the tyrannical regimes of the past, they are philosophically akin to the authority invoked by Roman emperors to torture suspected traitors, the Inquisition's forcible unmasking of heretics to save all from eternal damnation, and even the totalitarian temptation to eliminate all dissent in the name of the Revolution.

The threat posed by those who use terrorism to achieve their ends is real. But as the history of torture demonstrates, once torture becomes acceptable, it ensnares an ever-widening circle of victims. It has been nearly 250 years since Cesare Beccaria's *On Crimes and Punishments* helped ignite a broad social movement whose message still resonates today. For too long the spiritual heirs of Beccaria have been complacent in the promise of international law to end all torture. More is needed to win the hearts and minds of the public and bring this sad history to an end.

2

MORAL PROHIBITION AT A PRICE

Michael Ignatieff

Michael Ignatieff is Carr Professor of Human Rights Practice at the Kennedy School of Government, Harvard University, and Director of the Carr Center. He is also author of The Lesser Evil: Political Ethics in an Age of Terror (Princeton University Press, 2004). *In this piece, he assesses the moral arguments around the absolute and unconditional ban on both torture and coercive interrogation and the trade-offs we potentially make by forswearing these policies.*

It is difficult to think about torture honestly. In a recent article on the interrogation techniques employed by the United States, the writer Mark Bowden observed that few "moral imperatives make such sense on a large scale, but break down so dramatically in the particular."[1] The moral imperative—do not torture, anytime, anywhere, in any circumstances—is mandated by the UN Convention against Torture. "No exceptional circumstances whatsoever, whether a state of war or a threat of war, internal political instability or any other public emergency," says the Convention, can "be invoked as a justification of torture."[2] The fact that terrorists themselves torture—i.e., that we face enemies who do not observe the Torture Convention—does not change these moral imperatives. Our compliance should not depend on reciprocity, on whether our enemies observe these rules or not.

As long as we stay on the high moral ground of unconditional moral prohibition, we seem to know where we are. Problems begin, as Mark

Bowden observes, when we descend into the particular, when we ask what exactly counts as torture.

Since no state wants to be seen as torturing suspects but all states want to be able to extract information to protect their citizens, the key practical question for states is whether they can use methods of coercive interrogation that do not qualify as torture. When the Torture Convention was ratified by the U.S. Senate in 1994, maintaining a meaningful distinction between coercive but lawful interrogation and outright torture was a central concern. The Senate ratified the Convention on the understanding that torture should be reserved for *"severe* physical or mental pain or suffering" resulting in *"prolonged* mental harm."[3] Once the war on terror began, the parsing of the Convention went still further. In the now notorious memos submitted by the Office of Legal Counsel to the Defense Secretary to the White House in the beginning of 2002, these definitions were stretched to the point that the threshold for torture "must be equivalent to the pain accompanying serious physical injury, such as organ failure, impairment of bodily function or even death."[4] Any physical abuse below that standard counted as "coercive interrogation." Some forms of coercive interrogation, the lawyers admitted, might not be torture, but they would still be defined as "inhuman and degrading treatment."

When the European Court of Human Rights investigated British interrogation practices in Northern Ireland in 1978, they concluded that a range of painful practices constituted inhuman and degrading practice even if they did not qualify as torture.[5] When the Israeli Supreme Court ruled against Israeli interrogation techniques in 1999—techniques that included holding suspects in painful positions with hoods, and vigorously shaking the head and shoulders—they also ruled against them as inhuman and degrading, but not as torture.[6]

There is thus a conceptual and practical distinction between torture and coercive interrogation. There is a further distinction—at least in theory—between methods of coercive interrogation that are lawful and permissible and those that may be inhuman and degrading. While this distinction exists in theory, most human rights activists would deny that such a distinction can be maintained or observed in practice.

Human rights activists accept that in combating terrorists, reliable information is essential, and that interrogation is a central feature of any counterterrorist strategy. Kenneth Roth, the executive director of Human Rights Watch, argues that "respect for the Geneva Conventions does not preclude vigorously interrogating detainees about a limitless range of topics."[7] What work is the word "vigorously" doing in this sentence? It is intended to make it clear that a human rights defender takes seriously the necessity of getting from detainees real information that may prevent future terrorist attacks. But what, in specific terms, might "vigorous" interrogation actually entail? Clearly, Ken Roth and anyone else who cares about human rights wants absolutely to exclude any form of abuse. But what exactly counts as abuse in a "vigorous" interrogation?

In order to prevent vigorous interrogation from slipping down any slope, human rights activists want to collapse the distinction between "coercive interrogation" and "torture," and to maintain that any physical or psychological coercion in interrogation should be banned. But there does remain a significant distinction (significant, that is, to the victim) between the two. As legal theorist Richard Posner has argued, "almost all official interrogation is coercive, yet not all coercive interrogation would be called 'torture' by any competent user of the English language."[8] As the philosopher Jean Bethke Elshtain has written, "when human rights groups label 'unpleasant or disadvantageous treatment of any kind' torture . . . they fail to discriminate between cases," for example, between "sleep deprivation and amputation or burning or some other horror."[9]

Clear thinking about torture, therefore, is not served by collapsing the distinction between coercive interrogation and torture. Both may be repugnant, but repugnance does not make them into the same thing.

If coercion and torture are on a moral continuum, at what point on the continuum, to use the words of Richard Posner, does queasiness turn to revulsion? Vigorous interrogation might mean lengthy, exhausting, harassing exchanges with interrogators. Provided that there is no physical contact between interrogator and subject, no deprivation of food or water harmful to health, this might qualify as lawful interrogation. But at every ratchet of coercion, moral problems occur. Sleep deprivation will not leave physical or even permanent psychological scars, but as Menachem Begin, who was interrogated in Soviet Russia, remembered, "anyone who has experienced this desire [for sleep] knows that not even hunger or thirst are comparable to it."[10]

It might be lawful to deceive a subject under interrogation, by stating or implying that all of their associates are already in detention when they are still at large. But other forms of deception can inflict excruciating psychological anguish. Threatening a subject with the imminent death or torture of those dearest to them may not leave any physical marks, but it rightly constitutes torture, not just coercion, in even the U.S. Senate's definition.

Both the philosopher Jean Elshtain and Richard Posner have argued against the moral perfectionism that elides the distinction between coercion and torture and have stressed the cruel if regrettable necessity of using coercive methods on a small category of terrorists who may have information vital to saving the lives of innocent people. Posner justifies coercive interrogation on utilitarian grounds: saving the lives of many counts more, in moral terms, than abusing the body and dignity of a single individual. Elshtain justifies coercive interrogation using a complex moral calculus of "dirty hands": good consequences cannot justify bad acts, but bad acts are sometimes tragically necessary.[11] The acts remain bad, and the person must accept the moral opprobrium and not seek to excuse the inexcusable with the justifications of necessity.

My own work on "lesser evils" brings me close to the Elshtain position—in that I agree with her that necessity may require the commission of bad acts, which necessity, nevertheless, cannot absolve of their morally problematic character—but I still have a problem. If one enumerates the forms of coercive interrogation that have been judged to be inhuman and degrading by the Israeli and the European Courts—hooding, holding subjects in painful positions, exposing them to cold or heat or earsplitting noise—these techniques also seem unacceptable, though at a lower threshold of awfulness than torture. Like Elshtain, I am willing to get my hands dirty, but unlike her, I have practical difficulty enumerating a list of properly coercive techniques that I would be willing to have a democratic society inflict in my name. While I can envisage interrogations that deceive subjects—for example, by pretending to have full knowledge of their networks—I could not approve the deception of threatening either them or their relatives with imminent death. I could envisage withholding sleep, but not the radical sleep deprivation of which Menachem Begin speaks. I could envisage interrogations that disorient and isolate subjects, but I cannot envisage accepting ones that bombard subjects with painful noise or that withhold from them all contact with medical or legal personnel. I accept that a slap is not the same thing as a beating, but I still don't want interrogators to slap detainees, because I cannot see how to prevent the occasional slap deteriorating into a regular practice of beating. The issue is not, as Elshtain implies, that I care overmuch about my own moral purity but rather that I cannot see any clear way to manage coercive interrogation institutionally so that it does not degenerate into torture.

On the issue of regulation, there are those—Professor Alan Dershowitz, for example—who believe that banning torture and coercion outright is unrealistic. Instead the practice should be regulated by court warrants.[12] Judicialization of torture, in my view, would lead to its "banalization," to torture becoming routine rather than an emergency exception. I would take a similar position on coercive interrogation techniques involving stress and duress, physical abuse, psychologically damaging sleep deprivation, and so on. A position in favor of outright prohibition of both torture and coercive interrogation has gained strength from the abuses at Abu Ghraib and from the memos of the Office of Legal Counsel and the White House parsing the Torture Convention into permission for coercive interrogation. It seems clear from the dire experience of Abu Ghraib that outright prohibition of both torture and coercive interrogation is the only way to proceed. Clear rules for interrogations, with clear penalties in the Uniform Code of Military Justice, should be mandatory.

Absolute prohibition, however, is easy. Enforcement is hard, and even rules and punishment for infraction are not enough. The crucial element of enforcement of any set of rules and procedures against abuse of detainees is habeas corpus, the legal requirement of any detaining power in a democracy to produce detainees before a court of law and justify detention to a duly appointed legal authority. As long as the United States—or any state, for that matter—has the power to detain at pleasure and in secret, abuse of detainees is inevitable. International pressure, domestic mobilization, and finally Congressional legislation are all necessary to stop the practice of "ghost detainees": detainees held outside the United States, inside the United States, or in third countries, whose identities remain concealed. It should be mandatory that every single detainee held by the United States, whether a citizen or not, be publicly known. If operational necessity—keeping the enemy from knowing who is in our custody—requires that their names be kept secret, disclosure of their names to Congress and the courts can be undertaken *in camera*. It should also be mandatory that every detainee of the United States, whether citizen or not, whether held onshore or offshore, should have habeas corpus access to U.S. federal court, together with the legal capacity to make representations to that court about treatment and detention. Detention should be limited by law, and detainees who cannot be charged or lawfully detained as prisoners of war should be released. Detainees should not be deported to countries where torture is known to occur. Until recently, the British detained terrorist suspects in British prisons rather than deport them to countries where they might be tortured upon their return. Following House of Lords rulings critical of the practice of indefinite incarceration, the British government is proposing to keep these suspects under house arrest. This strikes me as a lesser evil than rendition.

I am not so naïve as to suppose that federal court review of detention will always provide effective remedies for detainees. Evidence of the impact of recent Supreme Court rulings and federal court rulings on the tribunal review process at Guantánamo, and also on ordinary treatment of the detainees, does suggest, however, that court review and access, however imperfect, is the only reliable way to keep detention under the rule of law.

So I end up supporting an absolute and unconditional ban on both torture and those forms of coercive interrogation that involve stress and duress, and I believe that enforcement of such a ban should be up to the military justice system plus the federal courts. I also believe that the training of interrogators can be improved by executive order and that the training must rigorously exclude stress-and-duress methods.

Two significant problems remain. First of all, there is the problem of the exceptional case, one where lives can be saved by the application of physical methods that amount to torture. "Ticking bomb cases" cannot be wished away. They might arise, especially in connection with a weapons-of-mass-destruction threat against an American or European city. An outright ban on torture and coercive interrogation in these cases leaves a conscientious security officer with little choice but to disobey the ban. In this event, as the Israeli Supreme Court has said, even a conscientious agent, acting in good faith to save lives, should be charged with a criminal offense and be required to stand trial. At such a trial, a defense of necessity could be entered in mitigation of sentence, but not to absolve or acquit. This is the only solution that I can see that remains consistent with an absolute ban on torture and stress-and-duress coercive interrogation. Let us not pretend that the enforcement of this rule will be easy or pleasant. Where the threat can be shown to be genuine, it seems evident that few legal systems would punish such a conscientious offender. But let us be clear: an outright ban on torture creates the problem of the conscientious offender. This is a small price to pay for a ban on torture.

Does an outright ban on torture and coerceive interrogation meet the test of realism? Would an absolute ban on torture and stress-and-duress coercive interrogation so diminish the effectiveness of our intelligence-gathering operations that it would diminish public safety? It is often said—and I have made this argument myself—that neither coercive interrogation nor torture is necessary, since entirely lawful interrogation can secure results just as effective as those produced by coercion.[13] There must be some truth to this. Israeli interrogators have given interviews assuring the Israeli public that physical duress is unnecessary.[14] We are grasping at straws if we think this is the entire truth. As Posner and others have tartly pointed out, if torture and coercion were both as useless as critics pretend, why is there so much of it going on? While some abuse and outright torture can be attributed to the sadism of individuals, poor supervision, and so on, it must be the case that other acts of torture occur because interrogators believe, in good faith, that torture is the only way to extract information in a timely fashion. It must also be the case that if experienced interrogators come to this conclusion, they do so on the basis of their experience. The argument that torture and coercion do not work is contradicted by the dire frequency with which both practices occur. I submit that we would not be "waterboarding" Khalid Shaikh Mohammed—immersing him in water until he experiences the torment of nearly drowning—if our intelligence operatives did not believe it was necessary to crack open the Al Qaeda network that he commanded. In other words, we must at least entertain the possibility that the operatives working on him—in our name—are engaging not in gratuitous sadism but in a good-faith belief that this form of torture—and it does qualify as such—makes all the difference.

If they are right, then those who support an absolute ban on torture and stress-and-duress had better be honest enough to admit that moral prohibition comes at a price. It is possible, at least in theory, that subjecting interrogators to rules that outlaw torture and coercive interrogation—backed up by punishment if they go too far—will create an interrogation regime that allows some interrogation subjects to resist divulging information and prevents our intelligence services from timely access to information that may save lives.

If there is a significant cost to an outright ban on coercive interrogation and torture, what can possibly justify it? Many of the arguments that human rights activists make in justification amount to the claim that torture shames their moral identity as human beings and as citizens, and that they do not wish such acts to be committed in their name by their own democracies. Other citizens in a democracy are not likely to value their own moral scruple over the collective interest in having accurate security information, even if collected by dubious means. It may be obvious to human rights activists how to adjudicate these claims, but it is not obvious to me. That is, I do not see any trumping argument on behalf of the rights and dignity of security detainees that makes their claims prevail over the security interests (and human right to life) of the majority of the population. The best I can do is to relate the ban on torture to the political identity of the democracies we are trying to defend, i.e., by claiming that democracies limit the powers that governments can justly exercise over the human beings under their power, and these limits include an absolute ban on subjecting individuals to forms of pain that strip them of their dignity, identity, and even sanity.

We cannot torture, in other words, because of who we are. This is the best I can do, but those of us who believe this had better admit that many of our fellow citizens are bound to disagree. It is in the nature of democracy itself that fellow citizens will define their identity in ways that privilege security over liberty and thus reluctantly endorse torture in their name. If we are against torture, we are committed actually to arguing with our fellow citizens, not treating those who defend torture as moral monsters. Those of us who oppose torture should also be honest enough to admit that we may have to pay a price for our own convictions. Ex ante, of course, I cannot tell how high this price might be. Ex post—following another terrorist attack that might have been prevented through the exercise of coercive interrogation—the price of my scruple might simply seem too high. This is a risk I am prepared to take, but frankly, a majority of fellow citizens is unlikely to concur. The important point—going back to where I started on the difficulty of being honest on this subject—is that there is a price, and opponents of torture and coercive interrogation should not pretend that it might not be high. Abstaining from the evil of torture is itself an exercise in moral hazard and should be justified as such, rather than as an exercise in moral perfection.

3

TORTURE AND TERRORISM

Painful Lessons from Israel

Eitan Felner

Eitan Felner is Executive Director of the Center for Economic and Social Rights and former Executive Director of B'Tselem, the Israeli Information Center for Human Rights in the Occupied Territories. In this piece, Felner examines Israel's experience with openly using physical coercion in interrogations and attempting to justify it legally, with important lessons for efforts today to legalize and regulate torture.

In a symposium at Hebrew University in 1987, the late U.S. Supreme Court Justice William Brennan said:

> The nations of the world, faced with sudden threats to their own security, will look to Israel's experience in handling its continuing security crisis, and may well find in that experience the expertise to reject the security claims that Israel has exposed as baseless and the courage to preserve the civil liberties that Israel has preserved without detriment to its security.[1]

This skewed view, expressed the month that the first Intifada broke out, can probably be attributed to the prevalent ignorance at the time about Israel's human rights record—until then, Israel had been very suc-

This article draws from a report written in 2000 by B'Tselem titled "Legislation Allowing the Use of Physical Force and Mental Coercion in Interrogations by the General Security Service."

cessful at constructing the myth of a "humane occupation" in the Occupied Territories. Or it could also be that Justice Brennan shared the blind spot that many American liberals have about Israel.

But as the stream of reports about the ill-treatment of U.S.-held prisoners emerges, accompanied by more documents by Bush Administration officials providing legal justifications for these methods, the more it seems that Justice Brennan's prediction—that Israel will serve as a model for nations faced with sudden threats to their own security—was unwittingly correct.

The growing resemblance between America's and Israel's approach to interrogation of terrorist suspects is not just confined to the striking similarities between some of the methods used—hooding, loud noises, sleep deprivation, exposure to intense heat and cold. What makes Israel's case so relevant to understanding the implications of American policies and practices is that for more than a decade Israel was the only country in the world that officially adopted the use of physical force in interrogations of suspected terrorists. Scores of governments around the world resort to more brutal forms of torture than Israel ever did, but the Israeli government's relentless efforts to legitimize illegal acts rendered Israel's abuses unique.

Torture continued as an officially sanctioned policy of Israel until 1999, when the Israeli Supreme Court took the courageous and long overdue decision to ban outright all forms of physical force in interrogation. The Israeli experience is also particularly relevant to the public debate in the United States about the legitimacy of torture against terrorist suspects.[2] The Israeli case categorically proves the fallacy of believing—as some influential American opinion-makers do today—that it is possible to legitimize the use of torture to thwart terrorist attacks and at the same time restrict its use to exceptional cases.

The Legitimization of Physical Coercion

The official sanction of torture in Israel stemmed from a Commission of Inquiry set up by the Israeli government in 1987 to examine the methods of interrogation used by Israel's General Security Service (GSS, commonly known as Shin Bet) against suspected terrorists. The Commission, headed by former Supreme Court president Justice Moshe Landau, determined that between 1971 and 1986 the GSS routinely used illegal means of interrogation against Palestinian detainees in order to obtain confessions.

Although the Landau Commission regarded the methods routinely used by the GSS during those years as involving "cases of criminal assault," it refrained from disclosing any details about those methods in the public part of its final report, focusing instead on the practice of GSS interrogators of giving false testimony about these abuses when they were challenged by the victims in court. According to the Landau Report, during this fifteen-year period, they "denied using any form of physical pressure on suspects when the GSS testified in court. In short, they simply lied. . . ."

While the Landau Commission strongly condemned this pattern of perjury, it failed to censure the actual illegal abuses of detainees that these false testimonies were designed to conceal. According to the Commission, these methods involving use of force "are largely to be defended, both morally and legally," on the basis of the GSS claim that in the fight against terrorism, a certain amount of force in interrogations was unavoidable in order to obtain crucial information that could save innocent lives. Therefore, the Commission was not concerned with the actual abuses committed by the GSS but only that they routinely lied about these abuses in court.

The most far-reaching recommendations made by the Landau Commission dealt with how the GSS should conduct its interrogations from then on. Instead of recommending measures aimed at enforcing the ban on the use of force in interrogations—a ban that already existed in the Israeli criminal code—the Landau Commission recommended that "the government should acknowledge that some measure of coercion is permissible, and then codify and carefully monitor the allowable techniques." This premise, that an effective interrogation of terrorist suspects is impossible without resorting to some kind of physical force, was based on its discussion of a hypothetical case well known to philosophy students as the "ticking bomb": A terrorist group plants a time-bomb in the middle of a city. The authorities hold a suspect who they believe knows the whereabouts of the bomb. The suspect will not cooperate. Should they torture him to extract the information and save the lives of innocent people?

The Landau Commission decided that in such circumstances the use of force in interrogation was the lesser of two evils.

> To put it bluntly, the alternative is: are we to accept the offense of assault entailed in slapping a suspect's face, or threatening him, in order to induce him to talk and reveal a cache of explosive materials meant for use in carrying out an act of mass terror against a civilian population, and thereby prevent the greater evil which is about to occur? The answer is self-evident. Everything depends on weighing the two evils against each other.[3]

Yet even in such extreme circumstances the Commission did not authorize the indiscriminate use of force. Concerned about the danger of sliding into the "despotism of a police state," the Landau Commission stated that "the pressure must never reach the level of physical torture or maltreatment of the suspect or grievous harm to his honor which deprives him of his human dignity."[4] Instead, it recommended the use of psychological pressure and of the use of "moderate physical pressure."

The recommendations made by the Landau Commission were approved by the Israeli government. Thus, Israel became the only country at the end of the twentieth century officially to sanction the intentional infliction of pain and suffering during interrogation.

The Case of the Ticking Bomb

After its publication, the Landau Commission report was harshly criticized in legal and moral terms. It is worth recalling some of these criticisms because they are relevant again. One of the most harshly criticized aspects of the Landau report was its endorsement of physical force in the "ticking bomb" scenario.

> A person seeking to justify torture, must know with great certainty that there is indeed a bomb (notwithstanding that no one saw it apart from the terrorists); that it will explode if we do not neutralize it (that the terrorists were sufficiently professional); that it can indeed be neutralized (that it will not explode the moment it is touched); that the person in our hands indeed knows where the bomb is located (perhaps he was not privy to the information, or perhaps when they heard that he was caught, they transferred the bomb to another place); that if we torture him he will provide the desired information (and will not expire prior thereto, or keep silence, or provide false information); that if he provides the information we will be able to neutralize the bomb (it will not be too late); and that there is no other way of uncovering the bomb (for example, by means of sophisticated electronic means); and so forth.[5]

As critics have pointed out, the required conditions are so improbable in the real world that even in a country like Israel, beset for years by countless terrorist attacks, such cases remain in the realm of the hypothetical. Michael Gross has argued that in fact for countries like Israel, facing organized terrorist groups, the "ticking bomb" scenario may be, paradoxically, the least relevant.

The "ticking bomb" argument only holds if we know, with certainty, that others besides the suspect will not intervene to move the bomb to another time or place, or to change the detonating mechanism. This is rarely, if ever, the case in Israel. There are no lone, Timothy McVeigh–like terrorists among the Palestinians, whose networks are sufficiently organized to keep on ticking with or without one captured member or another.[6]

Indeed, the "ticking bomb" argument had been discredited by moral philosophers and legal experts before the Landau Commission was convened. As Henry Shue wrote a decade before the Landau Report:

Does the possibility that torture might be justifiable in some of the rarefied situations which can be imagined provide any reason to consider relaxing the legal prohibitions against it? Absolutely not. The distance between the situation which must be concocted in order to have a plausible case of morally permissible torture and the situations which actually occur is, if anything, further reason why the existing prohibitions against torture should remain and should be strengthened by making torture an international crime. An act of torture ought to remain illegal so that anyone who sincerely believes such an act to be the least available evil is placed in the position of needing to justify his or her act morally in order to defend himself or herself legally. The torturer should be in roughly the same position as someone who commits civil disobedience. Anyone who thinks an act of torture is justified should have no alternative but to convince a group of peers in a public trial that all necessary conditions for a morally permissible act were indeed satisfied. If it is reasonable to put someone through torture, it is reasonable to put someone else through a careful explanation of why. If the situation approximates those in the imaginary examples in which torture seems possible to justify, a judge can surely be expected to suspend the sentence. Meanwhile, there is little need to be concerned about possible injustice to justified torturers and great need to find means to restrain totally unjustified torture.[7]

The Landau report was also criticized for justifying the use of force in circumstances that went beyond the hypothetical case of the "ticking bomb." This case presupposes a clearly defined and imminent danger. But the Landau Commission—and every governmental official who relied on the principle of "the lesser of two evils" when requesting approval for the use of physical force during interrogations—argued that the methods should be allowed not only when the danger is immediate, but also when the need to prevent it is immediate. In the words of the Commission:

> When the clock wired to the explosive charge is already ticking, what difference does it make, in terms of the necessity to act, whether the charge is certain to be detonated in five minutes or in five days? The deciding factor is not the element of time, but the comparison between the gravity of the two evils—the evil of contravening the law as opposed to the evil which will occur sooner or later. . . . [8]

This argument has a certain internal logic: if the method is morally justifiable, then it is justifiable, even necessary, to use it as soon as possible, because unknown complications may arise on the way to preventing the danger once the information is obtained. However, from the moment that the Landau Commission stretched the concept of the "ticking bomb" to include cases where the danger to human life is not immediate, and sanctioned instead the use of force in cases of immediate need, the exceptional case of the "ticking bomb" became the paradigm for almost every GSS interrogation.

In Israel—as well as in other countries faced with organized terrorist groups—the need to prevent terrorist acts can always be seen as immediate. Once it is deemed legitimate to use physical coercion against a terrorist who may be planning an attack in an uncertain future, it becomes legitimate to use such methods against any person that could be the "lead," however remote, to that terrorist. Where should the line be drawn between the person who planted the bomb and other members of the cell, between members of the cell and those in charge of the organization, between those in charge of militant activities within the organization and the political echelon?

The Landau Commission was also harshly criticized for failing to recognize that once the principle of "the lesser of two evils" is adopted, there is no logical or ethical reason to limit the use of force to "moderate" physical force as the Commission insisted on doing. Shai Nitzan, the state attorney for the Israeli government in many hearings of the Israeli Supreme Court (sitting as the High Court of Justice) dealing with the legality of Israel's interrogation methods, explained in court that "the degree of necessity dictates the degree of the methods we shall use," adding that *"even an act causing death, if justified, is acceptable."*[9]

Thus, the rationale offered by the Landau Commission to justify "moderate" physical force is equally valid for justifying excruciating forms of torture such as electric shocks, removal of organs, and rape when "moderate physical pressure" is insufficient to obtain information to save lives. All according to "the degree of necessity," in the words of Attorney Nitzan.

"The lesser of two evils" principle adopted by the Commission would also justify torture of innocent persons. Thus, not only would it be permissible to torture the person who placed the bomb, it would also be justified, when the authorities cannot apprehend the perpetrator himself, to torture the perpetrator's young daughter and show her excruciating pain in order to find him, provided the result prevents a greater evil, such as the bombing of a crowded building.[10] This view is so abhorrent that neither the Landau Commission nor any other supporters of an exception to the torture prohibition to confront the terrorist threat seem ready to adopt it, even though it seems to be a logical and moral corollary of their own positions. The Landau Commission it-

self, which supported the principle of "the lesser of two evils," emphasized the risk with "respect to the interrogation methods of a security
service, which is always in danger of sliding towards methods practiced
in regimes which we abhor." [11] But they all fail to offer any persuasive
case for limitations once they adopt the principle of "the lesser of two
evils."

The Slippery Slope into Routine Torture

Israel's experience implementing the Landau Commission's recommendations over a period of twelve years was a chronicle of a disaster foretold. In virtually every aspect, Israel's interrogation practices and policies
corroborated the predictions made by the Landau Report's critics.

First, the Commission's attempt to limit the use of force to methods
that would not amount to torture or other forms of ill-treatment was an
utter failure. Hundreds of testimonies given by Palestinian interrogees
to Israeli, Palestinian, and international human rights organizations, the
affidavits submitted by detainees to the High Court of Justice, and
the state's responses to petitions against torture give clear evidence of
the interrogation methods customarily used by the GSS. State officials
confirmed the use of most of the methods on various occasions. These
methods included violent shaking of the detainee (the interrogator
grasping and shaking him), prolonged sleep deprivation, hooding him
with a filthy sack, exposing the interrogee to piercing loud noise and to
extreme heat or cold, and binding the interrogee to a low chair, tilting
forward.

These methods were institutionalized, governed by detailed regulations and written procedures. A broad contingent of public officials
contributed to them. In addition to the GSS interrogators, a ministerial
committee headed by the prime minister oversaw the procedures; doctors determined whether detainees were medically fit to withstand the

torture; state attorneys defended the practices in the courts. Israel consistently claimed that these methods did not constitute torture or other forms of inhuman or degrading treatment. This is not surprising, given both the strong moral taboo that exists against the use of torture and the absolute prohibition against its use in every circumstance. Thus, in an effort to distinguish between torture and the methods of interrogation it adopted, Israel interpreted the prohibition on torture and ill-treatment in international law narrowly, applying it only to especially gruesome methods of interrogation. More recently, senior lawyers in the Bush Administration adopted a similar legal stratagem to legitimize various forms of coercion the United States has adopted since September 11.[12]

Clearly methods such as sleep deprivation, violent shaking of the detainee, or hooding his head with a filthy sack are less brutal than many interrogation methods used by other countries that routinely use torture. To many of us—lucky enough never to have been subjected to any form of coercive interrogation—they may in fact seem quite innocuous.

But they are not. In 1995 a Palestinian detainee violently shaken twelve times over a twelve-hour period fell into a coma and died without regaining consciousness. Dr. Gorm Wagner, professor of physiology at the University of Copenhagen, who checked interrogation subjects in Israel, reported: "I asked a former detainee to shake me as he had been shaken, but stopped him after three seconds. Twelve hours later I was still feeling the after-effects."

Other methods that do not involve direct physical force are more harmful than they may appear at first. These methods—such as sleep deprivation, the slanted chair, and the tying-up—were usually used in combination to increase the pressure experienced by the interrogee. At the same time, the interrogators isolated him from the external world, for example covering his head with a sack.

The degree of damage likely to result from these methods varied from person to person. But, taken together, the testimonies provide compelling evidence about the pernicious effects—both physical and psychological—caused by these methods.

Eventually Israel's High Court of Justice ruled that these coercive methods used by the GSS in interrogations of Palestinians are illegal since they are degrading and infringe upon the detainee's human dignity. Likewise, several international human rights bodies and UN experts condemned these methods as amounting to torture or other forms of ill-treatment. For instance, Sir Nigel Rodley, then the UN's Special Rapporteur on Torture, wrote:

> Each of these measures on its own may not provoke severe pain or suffering. Together—and they are frequently used in combination—they may be expected to induce precisely such pain or suffering, especially if applied on a protracted basis of, say, several hours. In fact, they are sometimes apparently applied for days or even weeks on end. Under those circumstances, they can only be described as torture.[13]

As also predicted by critics of the Landau Report, once the moral and statutory prohibition on force was removed, the slippery slope into torture went beyond the methods allowed by the Landau Commission. Throughout the years, the GSS regularly disregarded the constraints imposed by the Commission, employing interrogation methods that exceeded those allowed by the Landau Report and lying about them, just as they had recurrently done during all the years before the report was issued.

For instance, an official report by Israel's state comptroller about the interrogation methods used by the GSS from 1988 to 1992 concluded that "violations of the Landau Commission and GSS regulations continued to be widespread in the interrogation facility in Gaza and, to some extent, in other facilities." The report, which was kept secret for five years, also noted that "these violations were not the result of ignorance of the law but were done deliberately."

Justice Landau himself publicly said that he felt betrayed by the GSS for regularly exceeding the constraints on the use of force imposed by his Commission. "Apparently, there were double messages once again. There was the written code—the Landau Commission—and another, oral code in the field. And this is a terrible thing."[14] In October 1994, Yitzhak Rabin, then Israel's prime minister, provided a vivid example of the slippery slope when he acknowledged that the GSS resorted to torture to find the whereabouts of a soldier, Nachshon Waxman, who had been kidnapped by Hamas radicals. "If we'd been so careful to follow the Landau Commission, we would never have found out where Waxman was being held," Rabin said.[15] Waxman was killed during a failed rescue attempt by the Israeli army.

Human rights organizations do not know the precise number of Palestinians against whom the methods of interrogation described above were used, because the GSS and the state's representatives in petitions to the High Court of Justice have never responded to requests for these figures. According to estimates, in the twelve years after the Landau Report, GSS interrogators tortured thousands, if not tens of thousands, of Palestinians. In a radio interview in 1995, Prime Minister Rabin said that "shaking" had been used against 8,000 detainees.[16] The same interrogation methods were mentioned in hundreds of testimonies given to human rights organizations, indicating that these methods were not limited to exceptional cases. Indeed, it is clear that GSS agents used the same methods during that period of time against almost every Palestinian interrogee, indicating the existence of fixed interrogation procedures. The interrogators documented the methods used, including the length of time each method was employed. State officials admitted on several occasions to using the methods routinely.

In practice, torture was not limited to "persons who planted ticking bombs." It was not even limited to persons suspected of membership in terrorist organizations, or to those suspected of criminal offenses. The GSS regularly tortured political activists of Islamic movements, students suspected of being pro-Islamic, sheiks and religious leaders, persons active in Islamic charitable organizations, the brothers and other relatives of persons listed as "wanted" (in an attempt to obtain information about them), and Palestinians in professions liable to be involved in preparing explosives—an almost infinite list. In a number of cases, wives of detainees were arrested during their husbands' detention, and ill-treated to further pressure their husbands.[17] A significant percentage of detainees interrogated by the GSS were either ultimately released without charge or administratively detained, so it is difficult to place them within the rubric of "ticking bombs," even according to Israel's broad interpretation of the term. And apparently the bombs stopped ticking on weekends when the interrogators went home: GSS documents submitted during the hearing of their petitions showed that the sleep deprivation stopped on the weekend and resumed the following week.[18] Still, throughout these years, Israeli officials consistently continued to invoke the "ticking bomb" scenario to justify the methods the GSS routinely used. And a practice that was rationalized as the necessary response to address the exceptional case of the "ticking bomb" became common for almost every single interrogation of a Palestinian.

The Failure of Supervision Mechanisms

The Landau Commission's oversight mechanisms failed as well. Following Landau's recommendations, the Israeli government appointed committees and set up approval and monitoring systems. But supervision was extremely superficial, and, where the rules were violated, the authorities responded forgivingly, if at all. Prosecution of GSS interrogators who violated the permissions granted by the Landau Commission was rare, although the GSS deviated in nearly systematic fashion from the permissions granted. In the few cases that were prosecuted, the interrogators were acquitted or convicted of light offenses and given symbolic sentences. As before the Landau Report, GSS interrogators were essentially immune from prosecution for acts against Palestinian detainees.[19]

The court system also failed, until the landmark ruling of 1999 by the High Court of Justice, to prevent the routine use of torture in Israel. Over the years, human rights organizations in Israel made various petitions to the High Court of Justice, claiming that the methods regularly used by the GSS were illegal according to both Israeli and international law.

But until 1999, the Supreme Court kept away from addressing the general question of the legality of these methods, ruling only on petitions made by specific petitioners on specific methods. In most of these cases, the Court rejected petitions for injunctions to prevent the GSS from using physical force to interrogate the petitioners. In a few cases where the Court did issue an interim injunction when the interrogation was still being conducted at the time of the hearing, and the GSS appealed, warning that the interrogee had information concerning planned terrorist acts, the Court withdrew the temporary injunctions, allowing the interrogation to resume without restriction.[20]

Thus, the Israeli experience illustrates the implausibility of adopting the bizarre idea proposed by Alan Dershowitz, of authorizing judges to issue "torture warrants." Expectedly, the Israeli Supreme Court failed to intervene when the security services claimed that a particular method was necessary to avert a planned terrorist act. Only after more than a decade of relentless efforts by human rights organizations—carried out both in court and outside of it[21]—did the Supreme Court take a principled stand against the use of force in interrogations. In a landmark decision, an expanded panel of nine justices determined in September 1999 that the methods regularly used by the GSS since the Landau Report were illegal.[22]

Conclusion

Amnesty International has said that torture is the one form of violence a state will always deny and never try to justify. With the Landau Commission, Israel proved Amnesty wrong. Until the landmark ruling by Israel's High Court of Justice in 1999, it stood as the only country in the world that has legitimized torture, both rhetorically and judicially. Since then, there have been numerous reports of abuses, particularly involving the use of Palestinian collaborators, but there is no indication of renewed systematic torture as there was during the years that Israel officially sanctioned the use of force in interrogations.

The recommendations of the Landau Commission to allow the use of "moderate physical pressure," which were supposed to restrain the GSS in its use of force and stop it from operating outside the boundaries of the law, accomplished neither. As predicted by many critics, the report's recommendation had the opposite effect: by sanctioning the use of "moderate physical and psychological pressure," the Landau Commission ended up legitimizing torture and making it easier to extend it into a routine practice.

The failure of the supervisory mechanisms to prevent widespread use of torture was predicted and inherent in the framework established by the Landau Commission. Once the moral and legal taboo of deliberately assaulting the physical and mental integrity of helpless detainees has been lifted, the use of torture cannot fully be prevented.

The ticking-bomb case should remain where it belongs: as an interesting case for philosophy students to ponder about the limits of moral absolutism. As a basis for public policy regarding interrogation methods, it is disastrous, serving only to rationalize the institutionalization of torture.

The extent to which the Israeli experience followed a predicted pattern is remarkable. An article written fifteen years before the Landau Report foresaw Israel's story:

> The circumstances are so extreme in which most of us would be prepared to justify resort to torture, if at all, the conditions we would impose would be so stringent, the practical problems of devising and enforcing adequate safeguards so difficult and the risks of abuse so great that it would be unwise and dangerous to entrust any government, however enlightened, with such a power. Even an out-and-out utilitarian can support an absolute prohibition against institutionalized torture on the ground that no government in the world can be trusted not to abuse the power and to satisfy in practice the conditions he would impose.[23]

4

COUNTERINSURGENCY AND TORTURE

Exporting Torture Tactics from Indochina and Algeria to Latin America

Marie-Monique Robin

Marie-Monique Robin is a leading French documentary filmmaker and author. For her 2004 film, Death Squadrons: The French School, *she interviewed surviving French military veterans of the colonial wars in Indochina and Algeria and traced the inspiration, training, and intelligence they exported to Latin America's dictators, who tortured and killed thousands of their citizens in the 1970s and 1980s. Her contribution is a cautionary tale of what can happen when governments and the military are convinced that enemies are everywhere— and that any means may be used to fight them.*

The world is only now learning about the involvement of the French military in popularizing torture as a method of crushing insurgencies. During the late French colonial period in the 1950s, the French military developed repressive counterinsurgency tactics, including torture, in its battle against nationalist guerrilla forces in Indochina and Algeria. It later taught these techniques to Latin American security forces, leading to an epidemic of torture in the Americas. The French-developed tactics inspired such catastrophic programs as the cross-border Latin American political assassination scheme, Operation Condor. And the horrific teachings of the "French School" remain in use today.

Indochina

A generation of French officers who joined the resistance after France's humiliating defeat by the Germans in 1940 encountered the Gestapo's methods, including harsh interrogation and torture. Later, as military officers in Indochina, they faced a communist uprising that threatened to rob the French colonial empire of one of its crown jewels. General Charles de Gaulle's postwar government saw France's empire as an integral part of the country, and de Gaulle's insistence on restoring France's grandeur and holding on to its empire made him completely insensitive to the winds of emancipation blowing in the colonies, a political blindness that was to have disastrous consequences. Unable to consider a political solution suited to evolving political realities, France committed itself to a purely military strategy to solve its colonial problems. This military strategy carried its own implacable logic, wholly divorced from any of the moral or ethical principles that France, "the country of human rights," ostensibly championed. On the ground in Indochina, the French Expeditionary Corps included many soldiers who had fought in World War II or who had participated in the resistance, men who later went on to become captains in Indochina, and, eventually, generals. They were familiar with traditional wars—where there was a clear front and an enemy one could identify by his uniform—and with heavy armaments: tanks, planes, artillery, and so on. But all that experience was useless when faced with the charismatic independence leader Ho Chi Minh and his communist guerrillas, known as the Vietminh.

The French soldiers quickly found themselves embroiled in what they called a "rotten war," a war in which the enemy did not wear a uniform and was hidden within a civilian population that supplied logistical support. Basing their campaign on guerrilla tactics and a powerful ideology—the French soldiers at least knew a little about these from their experience as resistance fighters in World War II—Ho Chi Minh's foot soldiers struck quickly and unpredictably, spreading the tentacles of war across the entire territory. It was in this struggle, against an internal enemy who depended on an entire population and who resorted to political mobilization, that the French "revolutionary war" doctrine was elaborated, whose military response became known later in Algeria as counterinsurgency warfare. Specifically, it consisted of using some of the enemy's own methods of "revolutionary war"—propaganda, or "psychological action," for example—against him.

It was also marked by the search for intelligence about the enemy by any means, including torture.

Among the fathers of this new French doctrine were officers including Colonel Charles Lacheroy; Captain Paul-Alain Leger, an information-warfare specialist during the Battle of Algiers; and Colonel Roger Trinquier, the author of *La Guerre Moderne (Modern Warfare)*. Published in 1961, this work became a reference for the United States during its entanglements in Vietnam and Latin America. Perhaps the greatest champion of the emerging military doctrine was Jean Lartéguy. In writings such as *Les Centurions,* Lartéguy gave the new warfare a popular and romantic sheen.

It is true that colonial conquests have always been marked by abuses against the civilian population and that torture has always been part of the arsenal of colonial police practices. But it was only during the French experience in Indochina and Algeria that it came to be part of a global theory of so-called "counterinsurgency warfare," in which torture was the principal weapon.

The genesis of this new kind of warfare is the idea that the enemy takes the form of an invisible political organization hidden among the civilian population. One can know its leaders and its structure only by waging a war of information: by arresting masses of civilian "suspects," interrogating them, and, if necessary, torturing them.

This new doctrine of warfare also sought to turn the political weapons of the enemy, particularly propaganda, or "psychological action," against him. Spying and psychological action were used along with harsh interrogation techniques to "square" the zones where the officers sought to control the population and eliminate the enemy.

An entire generation of French officers adopted these theories and put them into practice in France's battle to hold its vital colonial foothold in North Africa, Algeria.

Algeria

During the crucial years of the French–Algerian independence conflict in the late 1950s, many French officers arrived direct from Indochina. They had experienced the humiliation of military defeat at Dien Bien Phu and the horrors of the Vietminh prison camps—experiences that helped remove whatever scruples they might have had as they began a new war in Algeria against an adversary that seemed very like the one they had faced in Indochina. The French troops even had a tendency to call the Algerian insurgents "the Viets."

In an interview for my film *Death Squadrons: The French School* (2004), one of the fathers of this new French doctrine, Colonel Charles Lacheroy, told me that he and his fellow officers had to forget everything they had learned at the war college and devise an entirely new manner of fighting for this new type of conflict. Indeed, from the beginning of the war in Algeria, French military leaders adopted the new doctrine at the nation's elite military academies. It was likewise taken up in academic studies such as the *Revue militaire d'information*.

The Battle of Algiers pitted the French security forces against urban guerrillas in a struggle for control of the city and also the country. The clash was a laboratory for applying the lessons of Indochina directly to a separate conflict. It ultimately became a model the French government exported. The doctrines of counterinsurgency warfare were openly applied during the Battle of Algiers from January through September 1957, when General Jacques Massu, the head of the Tenth Parachute Division, was given special powers, including policing powers. It was a unique situation in military history. From that point on, the soldiers were the only masters in Algiers, with absolute authority to carry out the war as they saw fit, without judicial or political interference.

Unhinged from political supervision, the soldiers also saw themselves as unencumbered by traditional norms of military justice. One note from General Massu finished by quoting Trinquier's *La Guerre Moderne:* "Our current laws are unsuited to dealing with terrorism for the simple reason that this form of aggression was never envisioned."

Torture was systematically employed in Algiers. Although the word did not appear in any official report, there were frequent allusions to it. For example, an order from General Massu indicated that when persuasion will not suffice, "it is necessary to apply coercive methods." It was during the Battle of Algiers that torture truly became the signature weapon in counterinsurgency warfare.

In *La Guerre Moderne,* Trinquier put it baldly:

Wounded on the battlefield, the infantryman agrees to suffer in his flesh. . . . The risks he runs in battle and the suffering he endures are the price of the glory he earns. The terrorist claims the same honors but refuses the same constraints. . . . He must know that when he is taken, he will not be treated as an ordinary criminal, nor will he be treated as a prisoner of war. Those who arrested him do not seek to punish him for a crime, especially considering that his responsibility for a crime has not been established. Rather, as always in war, they seek the enemy's destruction or submission. One will therefore ask him . . . for precise information about his organization . . . and a lawyer will certainly not assist him during this interrogation. If he parts with the information requested easily, the interrogation will soon be over. If not, specialists will have to tear his secret from him. Like a soldier, he must then face the suffering, and perhaps the death, he had hitherto escaped.

Trinquier's reasoning was simple: the terrorist, by virtue of his modus operandi—he does not wear a uniform; he plants bombs that kill civilians—does not respect the laws of war, so there is no reason why he should be protected by them. This statute of exception also makes it possible to justify the "disappearing" of identified militants or "suspects" too badly "damaged" by torture. One of the techniques used in Algeria, later applied in Argentina, consisted of throwing victims from a helicopter. When victims' bodies were found in Algeria, they were called "Bigeard shrimp," after General Marcel Bigeard, one of the architects of the French strategy in Algiers and France's most decorated serviceman. In Argentina, "subversives" were drugged with Pentothal, then thrown, alive, from airplanes into the sea in an operation known as "transfer."

After the Battle of Algiers was deemed over, the doctrines of counterinsurgency warfare were officially implemented throughout Algeria via the Centre d'entraînement à la guerre subversive (Counterinsurgency Training Center), dubbed "The Bigeardville School." Opened on May 10, 1958, in the small town of Jeanne-d'Arc, the school trained Portuguese soldiers on their way to Angola and Mozambique, Belgian soldiers headed to the Belgian Congo, Iranians working for the Shah, and white South Africans. In each case, as the documents make clear, the course of study was counterinsurgency warfare. One of the officers who taught there, General Raymond Chabannes, a captain at the time, showed me the handwritten lesson plan for his course on "interrogation methods." The words "torture" and "generator" appeared. But in the typewritten lesson plan for the same course, these words were replaced by "interrogation techniques."

Latin America

In the 1950s, certain Latin American military and political circles took a close interest in France's experience with counterinsurgency warfare. It was at the height of the Cold War; Western armies were convinced that World War III was already in progress and that it was being fought, in part, against communist parties on the home front. Foreign enrollment at the École supérieure de guerre in Paris grew during the war in Algeria, with a spike from 1956 to 1958.

The majority of the foreign students were from Latin America (24 percent from Brazil, 22 percent from Argentina, 17 percent from Venezuela, and 10 percent from Chile). These students even took "field trips" to Algeria to see the practical application of what they were studying. Among them was Colonel Alcides Lopez Aufranc, who studied in Paris from 1957 to 1959 and later went on to become a senior figure in Argentine dictator General Jorge Rafael Videla's entourage. Groups representing the children of those who "disappeared" under Videla's rule accuse Aufranc of being one of those responsible for the torture and assassination of political opponents. And in 1957, at the height of the Battle of Algiers, two French counterinsurgency specialists, both lieutenant colonels, were sent to Buenos Aires. Two years later, a secret agreement created a "permanent mission of French military advisors" in Argentina that continued to cooperate with Argentine military staff headquarters until 1980—four years after Videla's coup.

In an interview for *Death Squadrons,* General Reynaldo Bignone, the last Argentine dictator, confirmed that he and his security forces "learned everything from the French: the 'squaring' of territory, the importance of intelligence in this kind of war, interrogation methods. Our model was the Battle of Algiers." Bignone was clear, even on camera, that French instructors taught Argentine officers how to use truth serum in intelligence-gathering, "the cornerstone of counterinsurgency warfare." Likewise, General Albano Harguindéguy, minister of the interior under the military junta, and General Diaz Bessone, one of the dictatorship's ideologues, have both said that French instructors played a significant role in the genesis of Argentina's dirty war.

In 1963, a Spanish translation of Trinquier's *La Guerre Moderne* was published with a preface in which Trinquier wrote that he had not hesitated "to use torture to combat revolutionary war. Torture," the preface continued, "is the weapon of choice for use against the terrorist, just as the aviator's weapon is the antiaircraft gun and the soldier's is the machine-gun."

It is also interesting to note that Argentine military academies used Gillo Pontecorvo's film *The Battle of Algiers,* which won a Lion d'Or at the Venice International Film Festival in 1965, in their training courses. Intended to denounce the dirty war waged by French soldiers in Algeria, this pseudodocumentary was used to train Argentine naval officers to torture from 1967 on. But the story doesn't end there: the film was shown at the Pentagon on August 27, 2003, as relevant to the U.S. war on terror. It is also regularly shown to Israeli army officers.

French officers who had been counterinsurgency specialists in Indochina and Algeria campaigns reappeared in Argentina as elite figures within the Organisation de l'armée secrète (OAS), a short-lived French right-wing terrorist group. Colonel Jean Gardes, for example, who had been sentenced to death by a military tribunal in France in July 1961, instead arrived in Argentina in 1963. General Paul Gardy also reappeared in Argentina, as did Lieutenant Jean-Marie Curutchet, who was already infamous for massacring forty-one Algerians in 1957 when he was hired as one of the OAS's killers. Soon after they arrived in the country, the French veterans of the war in Algeria were offered jobs as trainers in the Argentine army.

Meanwhile, the Americans, confronted with the threat of communist guerrillas in Latin America and in Vietnam, also became interested in the "French School." One of the first was Senator John F. Kennedy, who went to Algeria during the war, then, as president, asked Secretary of Defense Robert McNamara to approach Pierre Mesmer, his French equivalent and an Algeria veteran, to suggest experts. It was in this capacity that, at the beginning of 1961, ten liaison officers under Paul Aussaresses's command were sent to work with the French military attaché in Washington and at the Special Warfare Center at Fort Bragg. Lacheroy himself had trained American officers for the war in Vietnam at Fort Bragg and at the infantry school at Fort Benning a few years earlier.

Over the course of my investigation, I found two of General Aussaresses's associates from Fort Bragg, General John Johns and Colonel Carl Bernard. They explained that the U.S. Special Forces "didn't know anything about counterinsurgency warfare," and that they learned everything, including the use of torture as the principal weapon in this kind of war, from the French. Notably, they explained that Operation Phoenix, mounted in Saigon in 1967, was modeled on a translation of *La Guerre Moderne* made by Robert Komer, a CIA agent, who became President Lyndon Johnson's advisor for the "pacification of Vietnam," and was sent to the CIA's station in Saigon. Operation Phoenix "was a copy, in every respect, of the Battle of Algiers," Colonel Bernard told me. "And it was terrible."

The School of the Americas, founded in 1946 in the Panama Canal Zone, specialized in teaching the techniques of counterinsurgency warfare, including torture. After Latin America's first "national security" regime installed itself in Brazil in 1964, it established a special forces training center in Manaus, "a copy of Fort Bragg." According to General Manuel Contreras, former Argentine dictator Augusto Pinochet's right-hand man, it was here that Aussaresses taught Pinochet's political police while he was the French Embassy's military attaché from 1973 to 1975.

Operation Condor

In a way, Operation Condor was the ultimate expression of the lessons learned from the French. "Our war was very efficient. In three years, the subversives were annihilated," General Ramon Diaz Bessone of Argentina said.

Established in 1975 by the autocratic governments of South America, Operation Condor coordinated intelligence activity between the military dictatorships of Chile (whose secret police chief Manuel Contreras set up the operation from Santiago), Argentina, Uruguay, Brazil, Paraguay, and Bolivia. Its ostensible purpose was to exchange information on the activities of government opponents and exiles. But the plan went much further than simply the exchange of information and intelligence. It led to scores of assassinations, the secret detention and transfer of exiles to their home countries for prosecution, and, in many cases, their subsequent "disappearance." The security forces of the governments involved worked jointly in one another's territories, often covering up cross-frontier transfers, kidnappings, and assassinations. Operation Condor was designed literally to exterminate political opponents, both in their own countries and abroad.

In Operation Condor, the techniques used in the Battle of Algiers were carried out on a continental level, with binational, even multinational, death squads. There was also the same obsession with intelligence and subversion.

The Future of the French Doctrine

Operation Condor was the gruesome result of the export of French torture and counterinsurgency tactics to other countries. But as can be seen from abuses in Abu Ghraib and other detention centers, it appears that the cautionary lessons from Latin America's dirty wars may not have been learned by the United States and the rest of the world.

In January 2002, during a special report on this subject by CBS's *60 Minutes,* General Aussaresses declared that torture was "the only way to make a terrorist talk about Al Qaeda." But General Aussaresses's old associates from Fort Bragg, retired General John Johns and retired

Colonel Carl Bernard, no longer share this opinion. In April 2004, before the scandalous photographs of torture in Abu Ghraib were made public, Colonel Bernard told me in an interview:

> At this moment in Iraq, we are turning to the lessons of the French—and we will make exactly the same mistakes the French made in Algeria and the Americans made in Vietnam. In the name of gathering information, we will use torture, which is not only immoral but ineffective, since information obtained under torture is absolutely not reliable. Torture is an expression of shortsighted policy. In the long run, it is a bad calculation because it is the best recruiter for the terrorists it claims to fight.

5

TORTURE IN LATIN AMERICA

Juan E. Méndez

Juan E. Méndez is the United Nations Secretary-General's Special Adviser on the Prevention of Genocide and President of the International Center for Transitional Justice. A native of Lomas de Zamora, Argentina, Mr. Méndez has dedicated his legal career to the defense of human rights and, as a result of his involvement in representing political prisoners, he was arrested and subjected to torture and administrative detention for a year and a half during the Argentine military dictatorship. His piece is a compelling first-person account of his own experience of torture as well as a stark look at the use of torture in Latin America.

The use of torture in Latin America is a long, sad history of savage barbarity but also of deliberate, cold cruelty and the hypocrisy of denial. History should record not only the specific attacks against human dignity perpetrated by vicious, pathological sadists but also the calculated decision made to promote or tolerate their use, by military, political, judicial, or other "leaders" whose awareness of the immorality and illegality of the practice is evinced by their refusal to acknowledge it.

Such a history would also be incomplete without reference to the heroism of those who refused to be broken, who protected their friends and colleagues even at the risk of their own horrible deaths. It would be especially incomplete if we neglected to mention the many courageous individuals and organizations of civil society that have dedicated efforts to denounce torture, to insist on accountability, and ultimately to ban the practice.[1] It is precisely because torture has been such a tragic fact of life that Latin America is a region where support for international efforts to eradicate torture enjoys widespread appeal.

Undoubtedly, torture became systematic and pervasive during the military dictatorships of the 1970s and 1980s, but it would be a mistake to trace its origins only as far as this dark era. In fact, torture was used by dictatorial governments as well as elected but authoritarian governments throughout the twentieth century, especially against political opponents (whether or not they embraced violence as a means to achieve political objectives). Socialist, communist, or anarchistic trade union leaders were especially at risk. It was extensively used in many countries against suspects of common crime, to the point that it became the standard operating procedure in the investigation of criminal offenses.

In the current democratic era, torture continues to be used, albeit in a less systematic fashion and perhaps with less intensity and cruelty than during the "dirty wars" against a perceived political enemy. There is now less need to destroy cells and organizational structures, and less fear that the victim of torture is an intelligent, dedicated revolutionary that knows how to "beat the system" if the torment remains at a bearable level. But torture continues to be the shortcut to the clarification of crimes, and police interrogators are more interested in immediate media-focused results than in successful prosecutions with scientifically gathered evidence.

They are also relatively immune from prosecution for torture, because prosecutors and judges believe the practice is so pervasive that it may be unfair to isolate a few cases. Judicial officials may also look the other way because the whole framework of criminal justice is heavily dependent on the police for even its meager successes in fighting crime. Impunity for torture may have begun in the dictatorial era, but it remains constant in the democratic era, despite a few valiant efforts and some signal successes in recent times. It must be recognized, however, that cases of torture do receive media attention in the democratic era, and that the exercise of free expression has yielded some useful instruments in fighting against torture. In that respect, it is highly probable that torture is now less intense and probably less systematic than during the military dictatorships. But it is still widely used, especially if the victim belongs to the poorer and marginalized classes, where cruel and inhuman treatment is less likely to arouse sentiments of solidarity or scandalize public opinion.

The failure of democratic institutions to do something about torture (in some cases, the deliberate complicity of demagogic politicians with irresponsible calls to *mano dura,* translated as free rein for police violence) has reached crisis levels. Citizen insecurity is the largest threat against democracy in Latin America today, and the source of streaks of authoritarianism that cloud the democratic debate, even as their failure at crime control is visible to all.

In August 1975, I was arrested by the Police of the Province of Buenos Aires and subjected to torture. Isabel Perón had succeeded her husband, General Juan Perón, after his death on July 1, 1974, and her government unleashed harsh repressive forces, both legal and illegal, the latter in the form of notorious death squads. In November 1974, she had established a state of siege (or state of emergency). On a dark winter night I was detained when I walked into a stakeout in a distant western suburb of Buenos Aires. My captors handed me over to an elite interrogation unit known as SIPBA (Intelligence Service of the Police of the Province of Buenos Aires). By then I had been handcuffed and blindfolded, and over the next two days I was transported by car to several different places in the suburbs, where I was interrogated under beatings and application of the electric prod (*picana*). I received five sessions of the electric prod in the course of what I judged to be about twenty-four hours, always by the same torturers and interrogators. By their voices, I guessed there were at least five and maybe up to ten of them, with distinct roles. I received very heavy blows all over my body, but they were not nearly as painful as the passage of electricity. They stripped me naked and tied me, spread-eagled, to a table or hard bed, and applied the *picana* to my genitals, my feet, my torso, my mouth, the back of my head, and my limbs and sides. For one of the five sessions, they placed me facing down and applied the prod to all those body parts plus my anus.

The *picana* was originally created to be a cattle prod, and when it is used on cattle, it is powered by batteries. However, the prod used by police in interrogation is smaller and more flexible. The machine makes a whizzing sound before it is applied, and the operator seems to be able to regulate the intensity or voltage of the discharge. The pain I suffered with each discharge was so intense that my whole body tensed up; many muscles ached for several days after my treatment. When applied in the mouth, face, or head, the shock creates the sensation of a blackout. Needless to say, I screamed at the top of my lungs; the interrogators assured me that no one could hear me. The torturer would let up intermittently to allow the interrogator to ask a question and me to answer. If the answer was considered inadequate, the prod was applied again, sometimes in a more sustained fashion. If I answered something they thought was a lead (as when I admitted to doing legal work on behalf of persons arrested like me) torture became even more intense.

In addition to physical torture, I was subjected to psychological pressure as well. My interrogators and torturers, as well as those charged with moving me from place to place, talked to me all the time, insulting me and my family and friends, threatening to inflict all kinds of harm. At least twice they pretended they were executing me by placing a gun to my head and clicking the trigger. All of this paled in comparison to the physical torture, except when they talked to me about my children (then three and four years old) and told me they would torture them in my presence. As it happened, they had not gone to my house; under the circumstances, however, I was under great uncertainty as to whether they would act on their threats or not. Amid the transfers I was twice examined by police doctors, mostly to make sure that I was not about to perish and could still undergo more torment. I was later dumped in a cell and left there for what seemed like another day or two, during which I had nightmares. They did not allow me to use the bathroom, and refused to give me water or food. Eventually they took me out again for a long drive, and delivered me to other officers in the Eighth Precinct of La Plata, some forty-five miles from where I had been arrested. The Eighth Precinct told a federal judge that I was being held there. I was held incommunicado for another eight days, but finally the judge interviewed me and allowed my family to bring clothes and food. At that precinct I was not mistreated; I was then transferred to the Unit 9 penitentiary, also in La Plata, where I would be held for the following eighteen months.

I was charged with car theft and possession of weapons, but the federal judge who interrupted my torture also cleared me of those charges, citing lack of evidence: the car owner did not recognize me even in a highly suggestive lineup, and the police reported that the weapons had been destroyed. Although the judge dropped the charges, the government of Isabel Perón held me in administrative detention under the state of siege. I tried to exercise the "right of option" contemplated in the Argentine Constitution (which states that a person held by the executive branch during a state of siege can choose to leave the country), but the government delayed the response for months, and in March 1976, when the military ousted Isabel Perón, one of the Junta's first decrees was to suspend the "right of option" altogether. I was allowed to leave the country into exile only twelve months later, in 1977, and only after intense pressure from abroad.

At Unit 9 I was placed with other political prisoners. As we shared notes about the treatment each of us had received before our detention was "legalized," it became apparent that virtually everyone had been tortured, and most of us with the electric prod. Some also experienced the *submarine* (holding one's head in water until the lungs feel like they will explode) or were burned with cigarettes, and all of us were beaten, with fists and sometimes with clubs. Through our families, we were in touch with the women inmates at the cellblock for political prisoners in Olmos, near La Plata. We learned that the female political prisoners had conducted an informal statistical assessment of mistreatment which revealed that in a few months in 1975 and early 1976, more than one hundred young women were taken to Olmos. Virtually all of them had been sexually abused during their interrogation, with the electric prod also as the preferred instrument of torture.

Comparing what had happened to other political prisoners revealed that the treatment to which I was subjected was the most commonly applied to persons in my situation, with the following exceptions. First, my family—with the help of my fellow lawyers—moved very quickly to inquire about my whereabouts, and within hours a writ of habeas corpus had been filed and a federal judge was directing inquiries to the police. This explained the need to move me from detention center to detention center, and probably also the five *picana* sessions in one day (on average, prisoners were held in secret detention for about a week, and subjected to two *picana* sessions a day). At the time, there were some judges who still lived up to their responsibility to control the police, and if they found an unregistered prisoner in a precinct, some police officers would be in trouble, especially if the unregistered prisoner bore signs of torture. It must be said that after the 1976 coup d'etat, these already weakened protections against abuse were eliminated: the practice of disappearances was meant to shield detentions from any scrutiny, thus allowing torture to proceed without limits in time or in methods, including murder and secret disposal of the bodies. Federal Judge Carlos Molteni, who had intervened in my case (and who had similarly honorable attitudes in many other cases) was arrested by the military on the day of the 1976 coup and held in Unit 9 for several years.

Second, I was arrested alone and not with other detainees. This meant that the interrogators could not play any other prisoner's statements or alleged statements against me. In fact, my interrogators had seemingly stumbled into my arrest and did not know what to ask me. They soon found through their files on me that, as a lawyer, I had participated in charges against the police, which made them particularly vengeful. But they had few if any clues as to recent contacts, so in spite of the pain, I was mercifully able to withstand the interrogation without offering any leads that might cause problems for others.

When security forces are allowed free rein, as in Argentina in the 1970s, they torture not to prevent harm or to gather evidence but to develop leads that might guide them in destroying the structures of the guerrilla organizations they are fighting. This means they will routinely torture every person they capture, without regard to guilt or innocence or to their significance as potential intelligence yields.

This belies the assumptions of those who advocate a "ticking bomb" exception to the prohibition of torture. Even if the security forces start with a relatively restrained approach regarding who will be tortured, the lack of results soon forces them to go into fishing expeditions. Since they are not in a position to know which of the persons they hold knows where the supposed bomb is placed, they end up torturing many in the off chance that at least one will give up some useful information. In turn, if the torture victim can sense the interrogator has no clue, it is relatively easy for him or her to withhold the information (as I was able to do on matters of much less importance). Torture is not just a means to obtain information; in order to be "effective" it must be a program for the destruction of the personality of the victim, and it must be widespread and systematic so as to spread fear in the population. In real life, those who advocate a ticking-bomb exception to the prohibition of torture must know that they are advocating opening the floodgates to torture of limitless cruelty and to the debasement of security forces asked to act in betrayal of the honorable traditions of their profession.

Lawyers who defended political prisoners, as I did in the 1970s, were a distinct target of "legal" and illegal repression.[2] At last count there are about 130 attorneys counted among the *desaparecidos:* those captured after the March 1976 coup and sent to secret detention and torture centers, never to be heard of again. At least ten of them were members of the informal network of lawyers that worked with me in 1975, including Roberto Fassi, the lawyer who represented me in court proceedings and secured the dismissal of the charges against me. There are more than 100 attorneys who, like me, were eventually "legalized" and spent months and years in administrative detention without charges. The number of those lawyers who left the country before being caught and then spent years in exile is impossible to determine but probably runs in the hundreds as well.

Given the scale of the use of torture in those years, a conclusion is inescapable: the tragedy of torture, arbitrary arrest and disappearances could only happen because of a total and deliberate breakdown in the rule of law. The "Western, Christian" government of the Armed Forces was considered "authoritarian" as opposed to "totalitarian" by its sympathizers in the United States at the time, presumably because it championed open markets and aggressively courted foreign investment.[3] In its exercise of authority, nevertheless, it was as totalitarian as any Nazi or Stalinistic regime: it controlled the press, often by the most brutal means, and made sure the judiciary was fully compliant with the regime's wishes.[4] The use of more than 300 secret detention and torture centers throughout the country was possible only when judges ceased to exercise their duty to entertain writs of habeas corpus and conduct unannounced inspections in police precincts and military installations.

Although habeas corpus was not technically suspended during the state of emergency, thousands of requests went unheeded, and the Supreme Court handpicked by the military failed to order the courts below to act as a counterweight to the repressive apparatus.

To be sure, this breakdown did not happen suddenly, nor can it be traced to an official institutional act of the Junta. In March 1976, the Junta dismissed a high proportion of federal judges, including all of the Supreme Court members and key appellate judges. All new appointees were made to swear by the new institutional order. After that, there is not a single case of an attempt by a judge to inspect premises under the control of security forces, and there are many cases of actual refusal to do so. But it is also true that rule-of-law protections against arbitrariness had been seriously eroded during the Isabel Perón regime, and the deterioration can probably be traced to even earlier periods in Argentine public life. On the other hand, a strong military government that vowed to step in to restore order did exactly the opposite: it destroyed the last remnants of checks and balances against despotism.

At the time, large segments of "respectable" public opinion cheered the armed forces on, even while liberal and democratic voices were silenced on the premise that they only aided and abetted subversion. Pro-government media outlets offered space to church leaders, "moderate" politicians, and leaders of establishment organizations of civil society, although in all of those categories there were also courageous voices that challenged the conventional wisdom. Support for torture and illegal repression was couched in muted or diplomatic language; public opinion on the issue was framed by arguments like the ticking bomb exception and appeals to extraordinary measures in extraordinary times. Just like in the post–September 11 period in the United States, government leaders and framers of opinion contributed to the creation of an atmosphere where torture and disappearance were tolerated and even encouraged, and where efforts to curb abuses were made unthinkable.

The atmosphere of permissibility was consciously and deliberately created, even while the leaders made certain no traceable "orders" were left as evidence. Perhaps they thought "plausible deniability" could be limited to exceptional cases and that covert operations are, after all, part of modern statecraft. In fact, they created a monster that grew while always being susceptible to control. The pervasive use of torture and the fear thus created among large sectors of the population, especially the least powerful, has left long-lasting wounds in the fabric of society. That is why it is important today to expose and stop the practice by U.S. forces of using "ghost detainees" and "extraordinary renditions" of prisoners to places where they can be tortured.[5] In Argentina in the 1970s, as now in the U.S.-led "war on terrorism," higher-ups shielded their subordinates from controls and inspections and, when pressure became strong, occasionally delivered up some scapegoats to try to show that the problem was limited to "excesses" committed by rogue elements without institutional significance.

The impunity that the armed forces created for themselves eventually led them to mistakes like the invasion of the Falklands-Malvinas Islands and the disastrous war with the United Kingdom that followed. This and other missteps forced the Junta to a dishonorable "forward escape" and a hasty transition to democracy in 1983. Argentine society led exemplary investigations into the repression of the dictatorship, starting with the commission on the disappeared led by writer Ernesto Sábato, which produced a stunning report in 1984, and the historic trial of Junta members that captured the public's attention in 1985 and 1986 and ended in life sentences for Videla and Admiral Emilio Massera, the head of the navy. Pressure from the military, including four attempted coups against the democratic order, forced the newly democratic regime to backtrack and pass pseudo-amnesty laws and presidential pardons. In 1991 it appeared that impunity would again prevail, but the relatives of the victims and the Argentine human rights organizations never abandoned the struggle. In the 1990s, the overwhelming majority of public opinion gave its support to the agenda for truth and justice. Eventually, citing international standards, courts found ways to declare that the amnesty laws were contrary to the country's treaty obligations. They initiated "truth trials," by which several federal courts received testimonies and gathered documentation to establish the fate and whereabouts of disappeared persons. Later, some courts declared the pseudo-amnesty laws unconstitutional and reopened criminal prosecutions against several well-known perpetrators of abuses.[6] At the time of this writing, there are dozens of notorious torturers and abductors in custody, including Videla and Massera. In one early case that has arrived at a conviction, police commissioner Miguel Etchecolatz, formerly head of SIPBA, was sentenced to twenty-three years in prison. He petitioned to be allowed house arrest because of his age (he is seventy-one years old), but the sentencing judge has initially denied that request citing the enormity of the crimes he committed. I have reason to believe, though no hard evidence, that Etchecolatz was the leader of the unit that tortured me in the 1970s.

The impetus for truth and justice is alive elsewhere in Latin America as well, in spite of the passage of time. In November 2004, President Ricardo Lagos of Chile received the report of a national commission on torture, based on testimony by more than 35,000 victims. The report complements the historic findings of the Commission on Truth and Reconciliation, also known as the Rettig Commission, which in 1991 described in painful detail more than 3,000 disappearances and arbitrary killings by the Pinochet security forces.[7] The current chief of the Chilean army has admitted "institutional responsibility" for the illegal and immoral practices of the Pinochet era. In Uruguay and Brazil there has been little official acknowledgment of illegal repression, except in some pointed cases or via the offer of reparations to victims. On the other hand, in both countries civil-society organizations have produced exemplary investigations and well-publicized reports that have contributed to awareness of the recent past in vast sectors of society.[8] In Peru, a report issued in 2003 by that country's Truth and Reconciliation Commission has contributed enormously to the literature of transitional justice and to the practice of nations overcoming legacies of abuse. In Mexico, the government of Vicente Fox has named a special prosecutor to investigate the 1968 and 1971 mass killing of student demonstrators and the practice of disappearances in Guerrero in the late 1970s. The United Nations lent support for landmark studies by truth commissions for El Salvador and Guatemala.

Truth-telling has been difficult but is now largely recognized as necessary, not only in Latin America but in many other regions as well. Prosecutions for human rights abuses are much harder, but they have also received a boost by legal developments in the international community, such as the creation of an International Criminal Court through the Statute of Rome of 1998, a treaty that has quickly obtained nearly 100 ratifications. The international community has also contributed to the legitimacy of prosecutions for egregious human rights abuses through the creation of several ad hoc and hybrid courts for the former Yugoslavia, Rwanda, Sierra Leone, Kosovo, Cambodia, and East Timor. Democratic countries like Spain, Belgium, France, Germany, Italy, Denmark, and the United Kingdom have demonstrated willingness to open their courts to the prosecution of crimes committed in other countries through the principle of universal jurisdiction.

Impunity needs to be broken in order to establish a firm basis for the construction of a democracy that is stable and long-lasting. Citizens must be able to trust their institutions, especially those created primarily for their protection. One of the major challenges of democracy in Latin America today is the perception of rising crime and citizens' insecurity. A principal handicap that Latin American democracies face in confronting this problem is the lack of disciplined, professional police forces that the citizenry can trust. There are many and varied reasons to explain why police forces are corrupt, inefficient, and prone to committing crime or protecting criminals. In varying degrees, however, it is also true that in all countries the police have been called upon, at one time or another, to participate in "dirty war" tactics under the direction of the armed forces. That experience has bred a sense of contempt for internal and external controls, and a belief that silence and complicity offer better rewards than whistle-blowing.

This context, in which police are feared and distrusted by the citizenry, makes it harder to obtain information and cooperation in solving crimes. Relations between law enforcement and the communities they are supposed to serve have broken down beyond repair in large areas of the Americas. As poverty, unemployment, and the widening income gap grow, young Latin Americans are driven to crime; the police respond with greater brutality. This in turn endangers individual policemen, since criminals prefer not to be caught and tortured and so they resist arrest and will often murder police officers to do so. To be sure, demagogues in the political system exacerbate the problem by getting elected to office with calls for *mano dura* (hard hand), anticrime tactics that inevitably fall into the simplistic solution of "letting the police-force do its work" and looking the other way at police abuses. There have been encouraging attempts at police reform in many Latin American countries, but the road toward a police force worthy of democratic institutions will be long and full of obstacles, not the least of which are those inherited from the years of illegal repression.

In the end, however, the growing respect for human rights among Latin Americans will win the day. It will not happen "naturally"; in fact, it will take hard, persistent work from civil society and among democratic leaders. Democracy faces many challenges in Latin America, and the legacy of human rights abuse is not the only one (and in some countries perhaps not the most salient). Dealing with the past, however, is essential to breed confidence in institutions so they can deal effectively with all other challenges. The eradication of torture is, therefore, not just an absolute demand of justice for the victims but also a moral and practical imperative for the present and the future.

6

TORTURE: A FAMILY AFFAIR

Héctor Timerman

Prior to being named Consul General of Argentina in New York in 2004, Ambassador Héctor Timerman was co-publisher of the Argentine newsweekly De-bate *and host of the TV program* Dialogos con opinion. *After leaving Argentina in 1979, he went to Israel and then to the United States, where he received a masters in international affairs from Columbia University. In this memoir-essay, he describes the anguish his family endured during the time in which his father, Jacobo Timerman, a prominent Argentine journalist and owner of* La Opinión, *a Buenos Aires daily newspaper, was arrested, imprisoned, and tortured by the Argentine Junta.*

"Of all the dramatic situations I have witnessed in clandestine prisons, nothing can compare to those family groups who were tortured often together, sometimes separately but in view of one another, or in different cells while one was aware of the other being tortured. The entire world of affection, built up over the years with utmost difficulty, collapses with a kick in the father's genitals, a smack on the mother's face, an obscene insult to the sister, or the sexual violation of a daughter. Suddenly an entire culture based on familial love, devotion, and the capacity for mutual sacrifice collapses. Nothing is possible in such a universe, and that is precisely what the torturers know."

—Jacobo Timerman
Prisoner Without a Name, Cell Without a Number

During the early 1970s, my father, Jacobo Timerman, the founding publisher of *La Opinión,* ran the most respected liberal paper in Argentina. When the most brutal dictatorship in Argentina's history came to power in 1976, his battles with the regime became a part of our life, and I was proud, though scared, of his willingness to publish the names of the victims of the Junta's repression. At the beginning of 1977, he learned from a foreign intelligence source that the military was going to arrest and probably kill him. He confided this information only to my mother, the managing editor of the paper, a young Jewish journalist, and me. After listening to my father, the journalist said to him that he did not understand why anyone who was still young, well-off, with a family and a beautiful, adoring wife would choose a fate close to suicide by remaining in Argentina. My father's answer was simple. He didn't want the anti-Semites in power to portray him as a cowardly Jew. He said he wanted to be like the heroic people of Masada, who chose to keep fighting and then to commit suicide rather than be captured. In the early morning of April 15, 1977, the army broke into our home and kidnapped him. That night was the beginning of a new, surreal existence for my family. Overnight, we had become the relatives of an "enemy of the motherland."

In the context of a society brutalized by the official discourse and propaganda campaigns against the supposed subversive danger that the relatives of the missing persons represented, we embarked on a search for my unfortunate father. In a pattern that repeated itself among families all over Argentina, my mother and I began by going to the police station the next morning to report the disappearance. The dialogue between my mother and the police officer illustrates how devalued a place a persecuted person and his family held in society at the time.

"I am reporting the arrest of my husband by members of the army. They told us we should come here."

"That's impossible; there were no antisubversive operations in that area last night. Maybe your husband got bored of you and went off with his mistress. Wait a few days; generally they come back when they get over their drunkenness. Had you taken care of your husband in time, he might have stayed. And I give you a piece of advice: forget about your husband and take care of your children, because they might be planning to leave as well."

After laughing at his own wit, he handed us the form we had requested and bade us farewell by saying "you can imagine what you can clean with this piece of paper." And he was right, since judges all over Argentina were rejecting the thousands of habeas corpus writs handed in by relatives at great risk to their own lives, claiming that the victims had never been arrested.

In general, each day the police would give us one or two other addresses to go to for information—not out of pity for us but so that we would go bother someone else. Every day we started the pilgrimage from scratch, going from place to place to listen to the same speeches on patriotism and the antiterrorist struggle.

At many of these offices they would ask us for money in exchange for information. It was always false, but we would pay just the same—sometimes out of sheer anxiety or despair, but always because we were afraid that, if we refused to pay, they would take it out on our missing relative.

One day, as I was leaving an interview with the head of the police, a person in civilian clothes approached me and said that he was one of the prison guards at the facility where my father was confined. He went on to say that my father was in bad shape on account of the tortures, that he wasn't being fed, and that he had fallen ill and needed medicines. When I refused to give him money, he started to shout at me that I was a bad son and that not even a terrorist like my father deserved the way I behaved. The shouting attracted the attention of other police officers in the building, who all insisted that I give money for my father. Imagine, they said, were he find out that you refused to help him. That was too much; I gave the man all the money I had as well as my overcoat. My father never received any of these things. This happened a few yards away from the office of the head of the police who had denied that my father was under arrest.

After forty days of this ordeal without our knowing if he was alive or dead, the telephone rang and my father was on the line. He told us he was now officially recognized as a government prisoner and that we could visit him. If thinking about someone being tortured is painful, it is not as terrible as to see the result of it. My mother and I waited two hours in the Central Police Department. We were allowed only three minutes with my father. He was a man destroyed, both physically and mentally. Saying good-bye as if for the last time, he told us he would never be set free and to reorganize our lives on that basis. My mother sobbed uncontrollably as she saw what had become of my father. She stroked him, as if he were a child, and kept asking, "What did they do to you? What did they do? Why are you so ill?"

A few hours before his call, the dictatorship had confiscated all of our properties, including the newspaper. *La Opinión,* the main dissident voice in Argentina, now became a propaganda sheet run by the Junta.

That same night our family had to make a crucial decision. Should we keep pressing for his release, having been told by the authorities that our actions could mean more sessions of torture and even his death, or should we keep quiet and hope that someday he would be released? For the first time we had to deliberate not only without my father's advice but knowing that he was the one who was going to pay the highest price for our actions.

For the next two months we were allowed to see him for a few minutes daily, and slowly he told us about the long sessions of torture with the interrogators obsessed about getting information on his relationships with other prominent Jewish figures and his Zionist background. Among the torturers were people who were very knowledgeable about

Israel and Judaism. Little by little, in short whispers, he told us not only about himself but about the fate of other prisoners he had met in the clandestine prisons, and the presence of Nazi memorabilia in the torture centers. On rare occasions he asked what we were doing about his situation, and was encouraged when we mentioned how his international colleagues and human rights activists were raising his case.

Nobody wanted to believe that the Argentine dictatorship was anti-Semitic. The Jewish community leaders refused to accept the reports of the first survivors who testified that Jews were tortured more often than others, and that Jewish women were raped more frequently than other women. Yet the proof was everywhere. In most torture chambers, portraits of Hitler hung from the walls, and swastikas were painted on them. The screams of the tortured were muffled with Nazi music. Official newspapers and magazines published articles about the difficulty of the Jewish integration into Argentine society and reheated the debate on the issue of double loyalty. Despite all this, Jewish community leaders could not believe the truth, and Israel itself maintained excellent political and commercial relations with the dictatorship. I gave the Israeli ambassador in Argentina a paper left behind by my father's kidnappers. That paper, titled "The Zionist Conspiracy," claimed that the leader of the Sanhedrin was Menachem Begin, and that Jacobo Timerman was his representative in Argentina. Just as in the Tsarist Russia of my grandfather's time, the Argentine Junta devoutly believed that the Jews wanted to conquer the world.

For the relatives of the tortured, it was very hard to go on living a normal life, going to one's job, enterprise, or university thinking about the people that were being thrown out of airplanes into the sea or tortured to death. Our reality was its own hell. When the media reported on the struggle against terrorism or the international campaign against Argentina, when people took to the streets to celebrate sports triumphs or entered a restaurant, laughing and kissing, it was impossible not to feel confusion, anger, and emotional isolation. Watching normal people doing normal things, we felt a bottomless sense of solitude and loneliness. It was even difficult to embrace my fiancée, Anabelle, thinking at that moment that somebody was hurting my father.

I asked myself if those who advised us not to inform abroad on the situation of the missing and arrested people were right, because by doing so we were endangering their lives. More than once army officers told me that each time I met with foreign journalists I was making my father's situation worse. I also had to endure the comments of well-intentioned people who voiced the opinion that the dictatorship's prisoners "must have done something" to be punished to that extent.

A few weeks after the first visit to see my father, we were waiting in line to enter the prison when a police officer came and told us that my father had been transferred to an unknown location. Again, he became a *desaparecido,* vanishing from the police headquarters. He left behind his Spanish and Hebrew prayer book because, we were told by the officer, where he was going he was not allowed books in a foreign language. Somehow I felt that the officer empathized about my father's fate, but perhaps I was just so lonely and helpless that I wanted to feel compassion from someone, even a prison guard.

For thirty days, we lived in terror, remembering the extent to which he had been mistreated during the first kidnapping. Then a call came from the police. I would be allowed to visit my father for three minutes each Friday. I had to report to the police commissioner's office in La Plata, sixty miles from Buenos Aires. There, every Friday, I would ask to see my father and the attending official would take down my phone number. I would then return to Buenos Aires, receive a phone call, and be told where to go to see my father. Each week it was a different police station, generally far from the center of Buenos Aires. I was allowed to speak; my father was not.

One of those Fridays, my little brother Javier broke down in tears and demanded to see our father. I was not authorized to bring him along. Finally, I decided to take a chance. When we saw my father, pale and skeletal and handcuffed as always, Javier took out his report card and said, "Look, Papa. I got the best grades in my class." My father wept. With the little flexibility allowed by the handcuffs, he signed Javier's report card. In the midst of all the horror, doing something so banal as that seemed like a huge victory.

In the middle of all the suffering and fear, there was very little community solidarity and a fair amount of hostility as well. Our family was ostracized. One day the Reverend William Sloane Coffin came to Buenos Aires. We had dinner together at the house of the rabbi Marshall Meyer. He proposed that we start a hunger strike at the gate of the government house. I refused. I wasn't scared of going hungry, or even of being chased away by the police—I was afraid to have to admit that the issue meant nothing to people, that we were just a nuisance to the majority who wanted to go on living a normal life, and that more than one of them would have stepped right over us, as if we were invisible. If our relatives had disappeared, then we, too, were immaterial in both senses of the word. I preferred to lie to myself about the effect of our denunciations and the repercussion of our efforts. It seemed the only way to plow ahead.

In another display of cruelty, agents of the regime would often wait until I came out of my house and then phone my family to report that I had been kidnapped. This behavior was not only prompted by sadism, but was part of a strategy to destroy all kinds of resistance. When I returned home at night, I found my mother in a state of terror, thinking that I too had entered the labyrinth of the missing.

At twenty-two years old, the thing I craved most was the normal intimacy of being with Anabelle. One night I told my mother that Anabelle and I would spend the night in my studio apartment, located in a modest neighborhood nearby. It had been given to me by my father when I entered university, and I had often used it to hide dissident friends who needed a refuge. I had not been living there recently because it had become too dangerous. Therefore, when the intercom buzzed at dawn, and I heard voices saying that they would call the janitor and compel him to let them in to my apartment, I was terrified and unable to answer. The agents of the regime often abducted people in the early morning hours, and I was convinced that I was about to be kidnapped. I told Anabelle that she should hide on the roof of the building until daylight came, while I went to face the kidnappers so they would not come up to the apartment and find her, too. I dressed in a hurry and went down to the lobby, certain I would be killed or at least that I would be facing my torturers. With a sense of impending doom, I opened the elevator door. There was no one in the lobby except my uncle and my brother, talking to the janitor. They were terribly worried because, during the night, they had received an anonymous phone call saying that I had been killed in a shoot-out. As my student apartment had no phone, they had been obliged to come there in person to find out the truth. I immediately went upstairs to look for my fiancée and found her crying behind a chimney. All four of us went home. I don't recall being either angry or surprised. That's what everyday life was like at that time.

Javier, at age sixteen, was the first one in the family to leave Argentina. As our mother lived in terror that something might happen to him, one day, without telling anyone, we took him to the airport and put him on a plane to Israel to live in a kibbutz. The image of his desolate face when he turned to look at us for the last time still haunts me. As we were returning home, my mother told me amid sobs that her father had left Russia in just the same way. The stories of anti-Semitism she had heard as a child had become the reality for her tortured husband and her uprooted son.

In April 1978, due to health problems and world pressure, my father was released from the military prison and committed to house arrest.

Our home became a political detention center. Two rooms were for my parents and me. The rest of the apartment was the realm of the two dozen police officers who guarded my father twenty-four hours a day. No outside visitors were allowed inside, and we had to ask permission to use the telephone. The building looked like a military garrison. Our co-op neighbors were very unhappy with the situation, but instead of complaining to the police officers or to the dictator, Jorge Videla, they sent a letter to my mother asking her to move to the country, so, they wrote, you and your husband will be more comfortable.

Just before the Jewish New Year, the American ambassador called me for one of our regular meetings, only this time *I* was the subject of his concern. He asked me, for my own safety, to leave the country. The armed forces were furious about my contacts with human rights organizations and especially with the American Jewish community. Since I didn't have a valid passport, I had to go illegally to São Paulo, where I contacted the Jewish Agency. As with many other Jewish dissidents, they issued me an Israeli laissez-passer and told me to go to an address in Rio de Janeiro, where "friends" would give me a ticket to Europe and Israel. These friends—I never knew their names—took me to the airport and made clear that they would be watching from afar until I showed the identity papers to the officers at the airport's first security checkpoint, but that if I were arrested, they would not be able to intervene. From that point on, I was on my own, knowing that several Argentines had disappeared in the hands of the local police while attempting to escape just as I was about to do. Once through the checkpoint, for the first time in more than three years I felt beyond the reach of the regime's henchmen. Unfortunately, my parents and Anabelle remained in Buenos Aires under their control. It would take fifteen months more until we were all reunited in Tel Aviv. Bowing to intense international pressure, the Argentine Junta finally expelled my father in September 1979.

As for our family, my mother and father never really recovered from the fear, the humiliations, and the insults with which we lived while my father was a hostage of the dictatorship, for the alleged crime of being a socialist Zionist. For my father, it was especially painful to see his wife waking at night with nightmares and gut-wrenching screams. After his arrest, a profound melancholy took hold of my mother, a sadness that never left her until she died, only in her sixties.

Bizarrely, in the early 1980s, my father's torturer, Ramón Camps, wrote a memoir about my father, in which he claimed that while under "interrogation" he was able to get my father to denounce the left-wing journalists who worked for him. Nobody knows what happens when someone is tortured except the victim and his torturers, but the fact is that the Argentine dictatorship responsible for the killing of more than a hundred journalists never did punish those journalists who were allegedly denounced by my father.

Recently, the writer and literature professor Tomás Eloy Martínez wrote an op-ed piece about my father in a respected Argentine paper. In it he said that my father "never apologized for his denunciation of radical journalists who worked for him during interrogation by the chief of police, Ramón Camps." Martínez used the term "interrogations" instead of "torture sessions," dismissing my father's testimony of those episodes. He builds up his theory of what happened entirely on the writings of the torturer. Not only did my father have to endure unspeakable pain, but now his surviving sons have to see how the torturer's version is accepted as true. Many years after the physical pain has ended, the moral consequences of torture still exist, and we are still responding to the torturer's accusations.

7

TORTURE SPOKEN HERE

Ending Global Torture

Minky Worden

As Media Director of Human Rights Watch, Minky Worden monitors crises, wars, human rights abuses, and political developments in more than seventy countries worldwide. In this piece, she spotlights some of the world's worst contemporary torture offenders and examines Turkey as a counterexample—a country that has made significant recent strides in reforming its torturing ways.

Torture knows no borders. It occurs in every region of the world today.

Contemporary global torture ranges from torture by regimes trying to maintain political power to torture in war and civil or communal conflicts to torture of suspected criminals with the goal of obtaining coerced confessions. The Convention against Torture and Other Cruel, Inhuman or Degrading Treatment or Punishment has been ratified by 139 countries, but as this review shows, many governments today ignore and in some cases brazenly violate these most basic prohibitions. Most countries try to keep their use of torture quiet, while a few others use torture in a more open way to send a message to government opposition or even to the broad public. Encouragingly, some countries with a long history of political repression are now repudiating their torturing practices as a result of domestic and international pressure.

Torture, by dictionary definition, has different meanings in different contexts. But in this review, it specifically refers to acts by a government official where severe pain or suffering, whether physical or mental, is intentionally inflicted on individuals for information, coerced confessions, punishment, or control.

Trends in torture can be identified across national borders. Most torture takes place in police stations and detention centers. It happens to political and religious prisoners as well as to suspects of common crimes. Torture is frequently used to force confessions from people the authorities think are guilty (thus freeing them from having actually to gather evidence and prove guilt), or from people the authorities know are innocent but want to frame. In the state security context, torture is used to obtain information, whether or not there is genuine information to obtain. Torture is also used to punish and humiliate prisoners and to show them that they are utterly helpless before the absolute power of their captors. Lazy or overzealous police take advantage of a climate where judges and prosecutors look the other way when torture has clearly been used.

Torture is used to intimidate society as a whole. It flourishes especially where civil society and monitoring groups are absent or straightjacketed, as in China and Uzbekistan. Put another way, if you disappear after a midnight knock on the door, are there lawyers and civil society groups who can press the government about your whereabouts, alert the media, and monitor your trial? In places such as Egypt and Uganda, civil society may exist, but government critics and the marginalized still face dangers. In the cases of China and Brazil, the countries' decentralized administrations and large size contribute to torture and abuse. Without independent monitoring and centrally directed government policy to stop abuses in prisons and police stations, there is little incentive to end torture. In fact, in many countries around the world, torture is rewarded—with promotions for the torturers and guilty verdicts for the tortured.

In her book *The Courage of Strangers,* Human Rights Watch

co-founder Jeri Laber writes of her work documenting torture around the world. "Torture is destructive to all of us—to the victims, to the torturers, to those who deny it is happening and to those who are working to bring it to an end. It forces us to imagine things that should be unimaginable, to think thoughts that should be unthinkable, and to read words that should be unreadable."[1]

Torture has existed for many centuries, in various forms, and in all regions in the world. The following cases illustrate torture in the world today, illuminate some current failures, and examine an emerging success in eliminating torture.

Uzbekistan's Unapologetic Torture

In 2002, two men were boiled to death in the infamous Jaslyk Prison. The bodies of Muzafar Avazov and Husnidin Alimov, both religious prisoners at Jaslyk, were returned to family members for burial. Avazov had burns all over his body, along with other marks of torture such as missing fingernails. The official Uzbek government explanation was that the prisoners were in a kitchen fight and the two men "threw hot tea at each other."

Today, some of the world's worst torture takes place largely out of view in the former Soviet republics, illustrating how torture flourishes where civil society is absent or under siege. Uzbekistan, Azerbaijan, Kazakhstan, Kyrgyzstan, and Turkmenistan all imprison political and religious opposition, control the media through bullying, and blatantly attack human rights monitors. In the dozen years of independence since the fall of the Soviet Union, Uzbekistan has proven to be one of the most repressive countries in Central Asia. It also has the most acute torture problem.

Uzbekistan has been headed by dictator Islam Karimov since he was made First Secretary of the Communist Party of Uzbekistan in 1989

and then named president of the Uzbek Soviet Socialist Republic in
1990. Karimov has put his personal stamp on torture by using it to instill
fear and to punish those who practice their faith outside of state-
approved Islam. In recent years, the simultaneous persecution of independent Muslims and harassment of human rights defenders has created
a climate where torture is widespread and unabashedly practiced in police precincts, in provincial departments of the Ministry of Internal Affairs, and at the ministry building itself. It is also common in National
Security Service facilities; in some cases, detainees are moved from facility to facility and tortured in each place. In April 2003, the United Nations Special Rapporteur on Torture presented findings from a mission
to Uzbekistan to the UN Commission on Human Rights. He stated
that torture was "pervasive and persistent . . . throughout the investigation process." Since 1998, Human Rights Watch has documented
twenty-seven deaths that appear to be torture-related.

Persecution of Independent Muslims

The government's campaign against Muslims who practice Islam outside of government-controlled institutions has resulted in the imprisonment of some 6,000 people, many of whom remain in prison today. The
overwhelming majority were arrested for peacefully expressing their religious beliefs. Religious prisoners are subjected to particularly harsh
treatment, including beatings, placement in punishment cells, and deprivation of basic needs such as food, bedding, and heating.

Common methods of torture used in Uzbekistan include beatings by
fist and with truncheons or metal rods, electric shock, use of lit cigarettes or newspapers to burn the detainee, and asphyxiation with plastic
bags or gas masks. Since the beginning of the Uzbek government's campaign against what it calls Islamic extremists, there has been a marked
increase in reports of rape and sexual violence, sodomizing of men in
detention, and stripping people naked. Torture occurs at every stage in

the justice process: before, during, and after conviction. It is used not only to coerce confessions but also as a form of extrajudicial punishment.

When prisoners arrive at a facility after conviction and at transfers, all are subject to what is called the "breaking," a gauntlet of guards with metal pipes and wooden bats. Prisoners fall and occasionally die running into these brutal beatings. After that, daily torture is used both as punishment for "deviant" ideas and also to encourage rejection of faith and allegiance to President Karimov. Family members in police detention are tortured in each other's presence, and threats of rape of family members are common. "Torture in Uzbekistan is so prevalent today that only grisly deaths in custody get attention," said Acacia Shields, author of Human Rights Watch's study of torture and religious persecution in Uzbekistan, *Creating Enemies of the State*. "Electric shock, suffocation, rape, and beatings are so commonplace they hardly spark any reaction."

From the state's point of view, torture works—to get coerced confessions, but not necessarily the truth. The wife of a man arrested for taking private lessons on Islam told Human Rights Watch, "My husband said that they threatened to remove his teeth. Then they told him to sign. They beat him on the legs, wrapped his legs in newspaper and lit it. In two days he told them what they wanted to hear. . . . They took him to Tashkent prison, [where authorities] refused to accept him because he was in such bad shape. But the police left him there, so they had to take him." Government torturers seek not only confessions and information but contrition. Even as President Karimov was publicly promising pardons to independent Muslims who admitted having followed the "wrong" religious path, police were torturing pious Muslim detainees to compel them to ask for pardons. The propaganda effort relied on the contrition of the accused to showcase the government's forgiveness and generosity.

Torture in Uzbekistan serves a variety of purposes: to terrorize certain elements of the population, to instill a climate of fear in the public more generally, and to break key leaders and members of these groups, uncovering their networks. "Once a person is tortured, forced to confess, and convicted, he is locked away for years, cut off from society and silenced," said Shields. "The government neutralizes its critics and makes criticism come at the highest possible price."

The most infamous era in Soviet history is the Stalinist period, but it is common among older Uzbeks to hear that today is "worse than 1937" in terms of torture and repression. "One word you hear all the time in Uzbekistan is 'arbitrary.' The social contract between the state and the people is gone," said Allison Gill, a Human Rights Watch researcher based in Tashkent, Uzbekistan. "Now there are simply no protections against an abusive state."

Torture is also used by officials as a means for simple corruption. Guards beat money out of prisoners or extort family members to pay them to stop torturing their loved ones. A UN committee investigating torture in Uzbekistan in 2002 confirmed the problem was so pervasive that every conviction since 1995 based solely on a confession should be reviewed. This would mean opening up for scrutiny thousands and possibly even tens of thousands of cases.

Today the government still refuses to hold police and security forces accountable for acts of torture, and tacitly encourages torture by broadcasting political prisoners' public "confessions" as tools of political propaganda. Judges routinely ignore torture allegations in court, while those responsible for torture have almost complete impunity. Human rights activists are persecuted and tortured themselves for speaking out about torture. Elderly human rights activist Ismail Adylov, who had been investigating such abuses, was arrested on spurious charges and then brutally tortured, every day, for a year and a half of his two-year prison term.

"Torture might happen anyway with the presence of civil society, but without monitoring, it becomes impossible to stamp out," said Gill.

China's Endemic Torture

For centuries, Asian rulers have relied on torture to preserve their power and silence their critics. Today some of Asia's most repressive governments—from China to North Korea to Burma—use torture both to deter political opposition and to keep discontented populations in line. By contrast, Asia once offered an historic exception to the then common practice of torture when, in the 1200s, the Mongol military leader Genghis Khan, more generally known for his battlefield brutality, outlawed all forms of torture in his empire. The success of that edict is not known, but in China under the dynasties that followed Genghis Khan's empire, torture was in wide use, particularly against those who crossed an emperor.

In traditional Chinese law, suspects were assumed to be guilty until proven innocent. The criminal code during the Ch'ing dynasty explicitly permitted the use of torture for extracting confessions from suspects who refused to admit guilt. As Derk Bodde and Clarence Morris explain in *Law in Imperial China,* the torture had to be within certain legally defined limits: "twisting the ears, slapping or beating, making the prisoner kneel on a chain, or squeezing the fingers or ankles with wooden compressors that are made for the purpose and conform to legally defined measurements."

When the Republic of China was founded in 1912, torture was banned as a sign of the new government's enlightened views on law and criminal justice. During the rule of the Kuomintang, and from the establishment in 1949 of the People's Republic of China under Mao Tsetung, however, torture flourished.

Torture for Common Crimes

Torture in China of many varieties remains endemic. Outside observers tend to associate torture in China with the country's periodic political upheavals and purges. During the Cultural Revolution, for example, intellectuals, senior officials, landlords, religious practitioners, and "reactionaries" were tortured and killed as part of a brutal "class struggle." What tends to be forgotten, however, is how ubiquitous torture has always been and still remains for everyday, nonpolitical crimes. A major reason is that torture is seen by the Chinese government as a legitimate tool for speeding the judicial process along. As the *2004 U.S. Congressional-Executive Commission on China Annual Report* found, coerced confessions, among other factors, continue to undermine the fairness of the criminal process in China.[2] Torture has been a feature of China's latest so-called "Strike Hard" anticrime campaign, launched in 2001, which promised an intense crackdown and quick trials of alleged criminal elements.

The need to get confessions—even coerced confessions—drives torture in China today. A fast confession means the police can proceed to the procurator's office, claim to have an airtight case, and be almost assured of a guilty verdict. Without a confession, police are faced with a harder and longer job of having to obtain and verify evidence. Security officials are rewarded with bonuses and promotions for doing the job quickly. "China's criminal justice system is based on confession," said Mickey Spiegel, Human Rights Watch's China researcher. "From the moment someone is detained, torture is a possibility every step of the way. It can be more of a risk to common criminals than for political or religious dissidents, since the latter may have higher profiles."

There are few checks. Those most vulnerable to torture are impoverished, uneducated people jailed on suspicion of crimes, who refuse to confess immediately (they are also least likely to have access to lawyers for defense). China prohibits independent domestic human rights organizations and bars international human rights organizations from areas where torture can occur. Despite both criminal and administrative laws against torture in China, no law expressly bars the state from using evidence obtained by torture. Acceptance of torture, the rewards it brings, and the presumed guilt of criminal suspects are serious impediments to change. An article in China's *Legal Daily* in 2003 concluded that torture persists because law enforcement officials continue to believe that torture is appropriate if the goal is to uncover evidence or crack down on crime. In Chinese judicial circles, this has been referred to as the "stinking bean curd" theory of torture—it "stinks but tastes good when you eat it."[3]

Torture for Political Crimes

More than fifty years after the establishment of the People's Republic of China as a one-party state under the Chinese Communist Party, the government maintains political control over its 1.3 billion people through laws against "subversion," "stealing state secrets," and "endangering state security." Although the Chinese Constitution expressly guarantees basic rights, such as the right to freedom of speech, religion, assembly, and association, many of those who seek to exercise these rights fall afoul of the state. Those vulnerable to torture include individuals wanting to expose corruption, political dissidents, religious believers, labor activists, Falun Gong adherents, and ethnic minorities including Tibetans, Uighurs, and Mongolians.

In Tibet, Chinese authorities continue a decades-long campaign against efforts to foster Tibetan Buddhism and develop Tibetan social institutions. There have been persistent reports of torture of Tibetan monks or nuns who protest during official visits or international inspections of prisons. A protest during a European Union delegation visit in 1998 led to eleven deaths, including those of six nuns, four monks, and a convict who sparked the protest by shouting "Long live the Dalai

Lama." Traditional Tibetan funerals, called "sky burials," revealed evidence of torture, including fractured skulls, broken ribs, and punctured lungs, kidneys, and other vital organs.

Some accused of political crimes suffer nonjudicial "reeducation through labor" which may include torture to get them to recant. Recantation allows the state to claim correctness, and according to Spiegel, "Those who recant are seen to have publicly transferred their loyalties to the state."

Although the phrase "Chinese water torture" has entered the torture lexicon, methods of torture in China today for both common criminals and political prisoners are more likely to include the use of electric batons, beatings with clubs, and the "airplane," where arms are cuffed behind the back in a way that makes every move excruciatingly painful. Torture is often designed to leave no physical proof, making it much harder to document. One practice is being forced to stand for hours on end. As a victim said, "After a while, you'll confess to anything."

The Chinese government does not justify torture, and in recent years has begun to punish those responsible for especially embarrassing cases. China's leaders know the torture problem needs solving if they are to be accorded the international respect they crave. But as an old Chinese adage reminds: "The heavens are high and the Emperor is far away." Even centrally directed political will to solve the endemic torture in China can be stymied by corrupt, lazy, and unaccountable local officials across the vast expanse of China. With no political opposition, a straightjacketed press, and none of the civil society groups that in other countries expose torture, prospects for reform remain bleak.

Egypt's Epidemic of Torture

Torture is widespread in the Middle East, both in the closed societies where conditions for abuse are greatest and in the region's more open countries. Most Egyptians live in poverty, and there is growing resentment of the entrenched, corrupt, and authoritarian government headed for nearly twenty-five years by President Hosni Mubarak.

Torture in Egypt has escalated since the 1981 assassination of then president Anwar Sadat. Ruled under a state of emergency since then, Egypt works to keep a façade of democracy and accountability, while tightly controlling the population and political discourse. The Emergency Law, which allows arbitrary arrest and indefinite detention without trial, creates a climate of repression and impunity in which torture has flourished. Torture is known or suspected to be the cause of close to twenty deaths in custody since 2002, including at least three cases from the dreaded State Security Investigations (Mabahith Amn al-Dawla) branch of the Ministry of Interior.

After Sadat's assassination by members of the radical Gama'a al-Islamiyya, the discovery that radical Islamists had also infiltrated the military was particularly shocking to the state apparatus. The State Security Investigations assumed unprecedented power and embarked on a campaign of torture and repression, rounding up thousands of political opponents—mostly Islamists, including many with no connection to violence or the advocacy of violence. An armed standoff with Islamist movements continued into the 1990s, and arrests of Islamists still continue. Many have been held without trial for more than a decade.

Victims of torture include not just political dissidents but also those detained in criminal inquiries, men suspected of engaging in consensual homosexual conduct, and street children. Common methods of torture used by police and the state security forces to obtain coerced confessions and convictions range from brutal beatings to electroshock to dousing in water. "Torture trickled down," said Scott Long, who has researched torture in Egypt for Human Rights Watch. "State Security set the example in the 1980s by going after Islamists with complete ruth-

lessness and impunity. Lower levels of police learned that they could im-
itate their betters. By now it is common knowledge at every level of the
police force that you can do what you want with detainees, whatever
their crime—and any consequences you face will be minimal. You
might even get a promotion."

One goal of anti-torture activists in Egypt is to enact protections that
punish torture as defined by international law, since Egyptian law still
clings to an inadequate definition of torture: the only form it punishes is
that designed to extract a confession from the victim. Torture to extract
confessions, nevertheless, remains widespread. For instance, since 2001,
hundreds of men have been detained under suspicion of having committed homosexual acts. Using new technology for old repression, un-
dercover detectives entrap young men through Internet personal
advertisements, arrange to meet them, and then announce they are
being arrested for espionage and haul them off to jail. With private acts
difficult to prove in law, police use torture to obtain quickly signed confessions to the "crimes" and to facilitate prosecution.

"Confessions simplify the justice process," said Long, who has monitored the trials of those who were detained for the "crime" of being
homosexual. "Police stations collect the implements of torture—electrical batteries with wires to electroshock people, butane gas containers
to suspend them and stretch their limbs, whips and hoses from water
pipes for beatings."

Yet beyond torture designed to force confessions, torture is practiced
in Egyptian jails and prisons simply as a punitive measure, to humiliate
and degrade prisoners, to remind them of their helplessness before the
state. Electroshock and other methods of torture are used to break political dissidents, not just to make them talk. Others are singled out for torture by stigma. A 2001 raid on a discotheque known as the "Queen
Boat," coupled with arrests of dozens of men on the streets, led to a
show trial of fifty-two victims that sent a message of fear and intimida-

tion to the public. Most of the victims were tortured simply because of who they were, or who they were accused of being.

Some forty prisoners were brought to the Abdin police station after 2 A.M. one day in 2001. They were forced to kneel. One man remembers, "The officer called Taha who was in charge really enjoyed seeing us beaten and afraid." One of the victims, twenty-two-year-old "Ziyad," said, "This officer who I think was a psycho came over to us. He started shouting abuse at all of us. He said to us, 'I want the *khawalat* to one side and the ordinary people to the other side.' He was silent for a minute. 'Of course, you don't have any normal people, you're all *khawalat*.' "[4]

Once arrested, men are tortured—beaten with whips or hoses, suspended in excruciating positions, burned with cigarettes and subjected to electrical shocks. In the words of one man, "They wanted me to confess to being gay and to name other gay people. Cigarettes on my arms. Electricity. At the police station, we were tortured every third day, with two days in between. There was fifteen minutes with the electricity. They took telephone wire and wrapped it around my fingers, my toes, my ear, my penis. It was connected to a kind of telephone they cranked up by hand to produce the shocks, and it was like death."

What does the Egyptian government hope to achieve by torture? The ability to torture with impunity is part of the mystique. Security forces routinely warn, "You will go behind the sun," meaning that suspects will disappear without a trace, into a place where anything can be done and no one will ever know. Even seasoned Egyptian human rights activists blanch when told someone has been summoned by State Security. Ministry of Interior officials confirmed to Human Rights Watch in February 2004 that there had not been a single criminal investigation of a State Security officer for torture, with only a few cases ever brought against the police. In Cairo in 2004, an Islamist died in police custody with nearly every bone in his body broken. The deputy minister of the Interior claimed to Human Rights Watch that the man died of diabetes.

During the 2003 anti–Iraq War demonstrations, many hundreds of members of the middle class—lawyers, doctors, and civil society activists—were hauled in to jail. Dozens were tortured. As a result, there has been a growing public understanding that though torture may begin in the shadows with the poor, the despised, those outside the range of social sympathy, it will inevitably spread. Middle-class intellectual opinion in Egypt is at the early stages of confronting the reality of torture and demanding change. However, a middle-class backlash won't in itself be enough to end torture. "The end of torture in Egypt will only happen with democratic change and fundamental changes to the system of justice," said Long.

Uganda

Torture has long been a feature across Africa's landscape. As documented vividly by Adam Hochschild in *King Leopold's Ghost,* European forces enforced slavery and colonial rule with beatings and often gruesome torture. During Apartheid in South Africa, Robben Island became synonymous with the torture of political prisoners. It is possible today to take a ferry out to Robben Island for a graphic tour of this once-feared prison, conducted by its former inmates. Elsewhere in Africa, torture remains widespread, and has become a signature feature—as with Sierra Leone rebels' cutting off of civilians' hands and feet—in some of Africa's most horrific recent wars.

"There are several categories of torture in Africa," said Peter Takirambudde, Human Rights Watch's Africa director. "There is torture during armed conflict, as in the conflicts in Sudan, in the Congo, in Burundi, and in the Ivory Coast. There is torture in less open conflicts, such as is occurring now in Ethiopia. And there is torture where the government seeks to silence or intimidate political critics, as in Zimbabwe. Finally, there is also torture in criminal settings to coerce bribes or confessions."

Across Africa, torture is used to deter and punish those who would engage in opposition political activities. Uganda in particular has a history of brutal military dictatorships that used torture as a way of enforcing nondemocratic rule. Today Uganda is well regarded among donors and the international community as having made strides in addressing HIV/AIDS and education, and improving the economy since President Yoweri Museveni came to power in 1986. But Uganda deserves much more scrutiny for abuses in custody and failure to take action to prevent torture. In northern Uganda, as two decades of civil war continue to devastate the civilian population, torture has intimidated the country's political opposition. The civil war in northern Uganda has pitted the Ugandan armed forces against the armed opposition, Lord's Resistance Army (LRA), headed by Joseph Kony.

"Museveni has been in power since his successful rebellion in 1986, and intends to run for reelection in 2006," said Jemera Rone, a Human Rights Watch researcher who has documented torture in Uganda in several reports. "Thus the security operations are very serious about brutally nipping opposition in the bud, including through torture. Torture in Uganda has come to be used by state security and military intelligence agencies, particularly in questioning opposition political activists and political opponents. Torture victims are almost always accused of membership or affiliation with opposition political or rebel groups, rightly or wrongly, and sometimes simply because they were denounced by enemies eager to use the state's apparatus against them.

In a 2004 report called *State of Pain,* Human Rights Watch documented the use of torture on political activists across Uganda by military, intelligence, and security agents. Methods include *kandoya* (tying hands and feet behind the victim), suspension from the ceiling while tied *kandoya,* water torture or "Liverpool" (forcing the victim to lie face up, mouth open, while the spigot is turned on into his mouth), and severe beatings with hands, fists, pistols, metal rods, and wooden sticks with nails protruding. Death threats are used, including putting a pistol into the victim's mouth, showing him fresh graves, dead bodies, or snakes. For women, the torture includes gang rape.

"Uganda set up a shadow sector of security operations to contend with armed rebel groups and crime waves," said Rone, who authored the *State of Pain* report. "But now the security system serves to deter political opposition by detaining and torturing supporters of the political opposition."

Another ghastly form of torture in Uganda is genital mutilation— sometimes resulting in castration—through kicking, beating with sticks, puncturing with hypodermic needles, and tying the penis with wire or weights. "It's ugly. The officials beat suspects, then they don't give them medical care," said Rone. "The castration often results from prolonged infection and rotting after beatings." The male genital torture cases that Human Rights Watch found are far from the only ones: the Ugandan Human Rights Commission ordered the government to pay damages to a man who was tortured for ninety-three days and who, in their words, "is not a man anymore."

In 2001 the Ugandan government established a system of so-called "safe houses"—unacknowledged, unregistered, and illegal places of detention—to hold people suspected of being criminals or supporting opposition politicians or rebels. Certainly this "safe house" system keeps those doing the interrogating safe, but with no oversight by the judiciary and no access given to Ugandan government human rights officials, these detention facilities abet torture by hiding abuses from scrutiny. People have been held incommunicado in such places with no contact with family members or lawyers, sometimes for months. In secret detention, they have been denied medical care despite severe injuries, kept blindfolded so they cannot later identify their torturers and interrogators, and threatened with retaliation if they talk about their torture. The constitutional requirement that criminal charges be brought within forty-eight hours of detention or the suspect released is rarely honored in these cases, so that fresh marks of torture can fade and the suspect can be coerced to sign a "confession."

"Thousands of people are swept up into a security apparatus that is operating outside the law," said Rone. "Uganda's security system has served to keep victims of the government's abuse silent and its perpetrators immune from punishment. Its legal system fails to provide any remedy, as charges are rarely brought and even more rarely tried. The accused have a choice between admitting guilt and being amnestied, and waiting indefinitely in jail for a trial to prove their innocence, which few can afford."

Cuba and Brazil

Torture in Latin America has a long history, which Juan Méndez eloquently outlines in Chapter Five of this book. During the Cold War, many countries in the Americas, including Brazil, Argentina, and Chile, had large state security apparatuses that picked up and tortured people thought to be political dissidents. In El Salvador, Honduras, and Guatemala, military and political violence have inflicted a great toll, including torture, on vulnerable civilian populations. By the 1990s, democratic governments replaced military dictatorships, civil conflicts wound down, and political prisoners were released. Across the region, torture has been greatly reduced from the 1980s, and today countries like Argentina and Chile are beginning to tackle their torturing pasts.

In Cuba, Fidel Castro's repressive machinery grinds on. Forty-five years after assuming power, the Castro government still persecutes dissidents for peacefully expressing their views. Cuba criminalizes free speech, assembly, and association; imprisons dissidents; and denies access to international human rights monitors. Human Rights Watch has found that Cuba's treatment of prisoners, with prolonged periods of solitary detention and beatings, violates the country's obligations under the Convention against Torture, which it ratified in 1995. "Cuba claims to hold no political prisoners, instead calling them 'delinquent counter-revolutionaries,' " said José Miguel Vivanco, Americas director for Human Rights Watch. "But the Cuban government's heavy reliance on prolonged solitary confinement meets the definition of psychological torture."

Elsewhere in the region, torture has receded, but, among the largest countries, Mexico and Brazil are places where brutal torture of suspected criminals and individuals from marginalized groups remains common. "Across the Americas, in most criminal investigations, the preferred evidence used in trials is still coerced confession," said Vivanco. "Particularly for the state police in Mexico and Brazil, there are structural problems that encourage torture." While the federal police may have more resources and training, at the local level there is little transparency or accountability to prevent abuses or torture.

In Brazil, Latin America's largest country, torture was commonly used in periods of severe political repression during the country's twenty-five-year military dictatorship, which gave way to civilian rule in 1989. Today it is in the criminal justice system, particularly police stations and pretrial detention centers, that most torture occurs. "To extract confessions from suspected criminals, police today sometimes resort to torture techniques that were used against political prisoners a generation ago," said Lance Lattig, a Human Rights Watch editor who worked in Brazil as a journalist.

Some of these types of torture include the "parrot's perch," where victims are suspended hanging upside down from a pole and beaten. Other forms include the "telephone," painful beatings on the ears, and beatings with nightsticks and/or the "cassette," a rubber stick with a metal core that inflicts terrible pain.

With waves of urban crime in recent years, Brazilian officials face pressure from the public to crack down on crime and criminals, but they often lack the resources and cut corners on investigations, leading to confessions extracted by torture. Moreover, hopelessly overcrowded prison conditions lead guards to use brutality to keep order. The marginalized groups that make up the vast majority of torture victims in Brazil, particularly those accused or convicted of crimes, enjoy little public sympathy and are viewed as possible public threats. State officials may feel that the public will hold them accountable if they don't crack down on crime—but that they won't have to pay a price for brutalizing detainees and prisoners.

One source of Brazil's torture problems relates to the country's vast size and federal governing structure. "Brazil is perhaps the most decentralized country in the region," said Vivanco. "In rural areas, the northeast especially, a vigilante approach to fighting crime prevails, which results in torture and even extrajudicial executions." Brazil's decentralized federal structure means that although there is a federal law against torture, the administration of those laws is local and subject to the whim of local officials, particularly in police stations, where abusive treatment remains commonplace. "It is very common for someone who is detained to be beaten," said Michael Bochenek, a Human Rights Watch researcher who investigates juvenile detention facilities in Latin America. "Police do it to get information or to punish for a crime that has been committed—they don't observe a presumption of innocence."

Reforms are happening in law, but lag in practice. Since the return to civilian government, recent administrations have been more willing to ratify human rights treaties and introduce human rights provisions into domestic legislation than were past governments. Brazil's antitorture law was passed in 1997, but a relatively small number of perpetrators have effectively been prosecuted under it. "The statute is hollow rhetoric for kids in most juvenile detention facilities. It's not enforced and has little impact on day-to-day conditions," said Bochenek, who has documented torture of juveniles in Brazil.

Thus to achieve the progress on the ground that has been achieved in law, several reforms must occur. It will take a long period of retraining and restructuring to change the prevailing culture within the police and prison staff. "Torture doesn't happen in a vacuum," said Bochenek. "It scales up from other abuses. When there is no effective outside monitoring, abuses of all kinds, including torture, are more likely."

Brazil does have independent civilian review panels, called *"conselhos estaduais,"* or state councils. But state officials frequently try to obstruct their investigations. In the state of Rio de Janeiro in July 2004, local officials defied a judge's order to allow an independent monitoring group to photograph inside a prison by throwing them out and confiscating the camera.

These monitoring bodies need to be more than window dressing. They must be expanded, granted unimpeded access, and given free rein to produce reports. Then states should act on the councils' findings. Prosecutors should be prepared to prosecute based on the findings of the state councils, and state detention authorities must accept responsibility for abuses they uncover. If the councils were expanded and given greater status and powers, and if enforcement catches up with legal reforms, the tide could begin to turn in Brazil in practice as well as in law.

Turkey's Turning Point

To those who say that torture is the natural state of mankind and that once entrenched, it is nearly impossible to roll back, Turkey is an important recent counterexample. Turkey was once nearly synonymous with torture. Human Rights Watch did a grim series of reports on torture in Turkey starting in 1983 that documented chilling stories of students, intellectuals, and government critics who were brutally tortured. The movie *Midnight Express* brought Turkey's torture into the popular imagination. But today, torture, once endemic in police stations and gendarmeries across Turkey, has been greatly reduced. The past five years have seen more human rights progress in Turkey than occurred in the previous five decades. Even the notorious Sultanahmet Prison, which until the 1970s held poets, writers, and political dissidents, has now been put to use as the unlikely venue for one of Istanbul's poshest hotels, the Four Seasons (where leg irons and torture implements greet guests on a wall in the main reception area).

So Turkey may be starting to come to terms with its torturing past. What was the catalyst for Turkey's torture turning point and how can those lessons be applied around the world? Key factors included international and domestic pressure, state withdrawal of support for torture, and very basic legal reforms. Conventional wisdom holds that the European Union accession process was the key catalyst, and indeed it was an important factor. But in reality, the momentum for torture reform was homegrown, and began in Turkey long before the EU process in the late 1990s.

Common from Ottoman days onward, the worst modern outbreak of torture in Turkey dates from the 1980 military coup, when a group of generals seized power, extended martial law throughout the country, and detained enormous numbers of people, including opposition politicians, students, writers, and artists, holding them in incommunicado detention for up to ninety days. Between 1980 and 1994, 450 people died in police custody, many with gruesome evidence of torture.

In 1984, civilian rule was restored. But by the 1990s, police and the gendarmerie were struggling to cope with illegal armed organizations, particularly the Kurdistan Workers' Party, or PKK, which was then posing a considerable threat in Turkey's southeast. Government security forces tried to crush the armed groups by any means necessary, making it dangerous to be a young man in Kurdish villages at that time. "Security forces' standard response to any PKK activity was to round up all the males of the nearest villages and torture them," said Jonathan Sugden, a Human Rights Watch researcher who has documented human rights conditions in Turkey for nearly two decades. Deaths in custody went up again markedly, with at least forty-five detainees dying in 1994. "Hosing with cold water under pressure, electric shocks, and rape with truncheons were commonplace methods, but what actually killed people was the beatings: brain injuries when heads hit walls, or chest injuries with broken ribs," said Sugden.

Reversing Turkey's Trend

With hindsight, the first concrete sign of progress toward ending torture came when Turkey ratified the European Torture Convention in 1988, apparently under pressure from a state complaint against Turkey in the Council of Europe for abuses committed since the military coup. Acceding to the European Torture Convention meant Turkey had to grant the European Committee for the Prevention of Torture (CPT) access to police stations for unscheduled visits, beginning in 1990. "It was to maintain diplomatic respectability, I think, that Turkey let the Committee in to monitor," said Sugden. "The authorities must have been certain they could manage the process, but in the event, they couldn't."

The reports of the earliest visits have not yet been published, but the deterrent effect of having possible outside monitors marching in at any moment was significant. Although the government technically had the right to veto publication of CPT reports, in December 1992, citing the gravity of their findings, the CPT stated without the government's approval that torture in Turkey was "widespread . . . a deeply-rooted problem." In response, the Turkish government shortened detention times and increased access to legal counsel, though police constantly subverted the safeguards. As the conflict in the southeast raged, deaths in custody peaked in 1994, and two years later the CPT made a further statement confirming that torture continued.

It was about this time that dogged domestic champions in the fight against torture began to have an impact. In January 1996, Sabri Ergül, a member of parliament, was alerted that the children of several constituents were being held in incommunicado detention. Ergül entered Manisa Police Headquarters unannounced: "I heard a cry and opened the door of the next room to find out what was going on. The young people were there. They were blindfolded and some of them were naked." Ergül contacted the media, and several TV channels showed footage of him hanging handwritten notices outside the police station saying THERE IS TORTURE HERE. Blindfolded, stripped naked, raped with batons, given electric shocks, hosed with pressurized water, and beaten, the teenagers who had confessed to their crimes under torture were found guilty and were sentenced to terms of up to twelve years in prison. Some were taken to the hospital with internal bleeding and psychological problems.

Until this moment, ordinary Turkish citizens had been able to tell themselves that the accounts of torture were just anti-Turkish propaganda spread by foreign meddlers. Here was credible confirmation that the allegations had been true all along. Ergül's revelations caused widespread consternation and public outrage. In early 1997 the government substantially reduced detention periods, abolished incommunicado detention in law for criminal detainees, and reduced incommunicado detention to four days for people detained for political offenses.

Another Turkish politician who was determined to rid her country of the taint of torture was Parliamentary Human Rights Commission chairwoman Sema Piskinsut. A medical doctor and parliamentary deputy, she formed a team that visited prisons and, by interviewing prisoners there, discovered the locations of secret interrogation rooms and torture equipment. A member of her team reported, "We have seen people who carry the marks of torture on their bodies. Doctors in our delegation proved with documents that a number of these people had been subjected to torture. Some of them still had bruises all over their faces, their eyes, etc. Since Sema Piskinsut was a doctor herself, she personally examined some forty female prisoners. We asked a prisoner who said he was harshly tortured in Urfa to speak about the place and the way in which he was tortured. The prisoner had difficulty in describing the interrogation room of the Urfa police department since he was blindfolded. Then we asked him to cover his eyes and to try to recall what happened. After some difficulty, he took us to the scene of torture. There, we saw the torture devices. The ground was wet, we saw mechanisms that made the prisoners subject to cold water shock, electric cables and wheels used for hanging people. We recorded and documented what we saw."

Sema Piskinsut turned out to be a tenacious foe of torture. She alerted the media, made a stink, and the public grew angry. She published a series of extremely detailed reports as official parliamentary documents. Other embarrassing revelations about the police and state followed, as did national public demonstrations against torture and corruption. "Sema Piskinsut was really offended that torturers were staining the reputation of her homeland," said Sugden. "With torture so thoroughly documented by a patriotic Turk of the political mainstream, the findings couldn't be written off or ignored." The press covered the grisly revelations, and the state had to respond with more reforms, including, in 1999, the institution of a system of police-station monitoring by local governors and prosecutors.

These incremental reforms began to add up to a significant system of safeguards. With greater scrutiny of police stations and a greater readiness to prosecute torturers (though still not to convict), eventually the result was a measurable reduction in the number and severity of torture cases.

In 1999, Turkey was rewarded for its modest progress by becoming a candidate for EU accession. It was the beginning of a virtuous circle as the EU accession process pushed reforms further forward. In 1999, the European Commission set a number of reform benchmarks for Turkey to be allowed into the EU, including combating torture. Movement was slow at first, but in 2002, an unlikely alliance of the media, the business community, trade unions, and human rights organizations sharply demanded more convincing reforms to keep the candidacy process alive. The government gave way, and the pace of reforms began to pick up under the current moderate Muslim government headed by Prime Minister Recep Tayyip Erdoğan. Since 2002, Turkey has bolstered press and speech freedoms for civil society, and improved basic rights for women and Kurds. In July 2003, Turkey finally abolished incommunicado detention officially.

The gap between law and practice remains, but progress is striking. Today, most detainees get to see a lawyer, and most are brought before a judge within a matter of hours. Since 2000, there have been no deaths in police stations that appeared to be from torture. "Even lawyers who are highly skeptical of the present government and its reform program readily concede that torture is down, and that their clients are treated significantly better than they were a few years ago," said Sugden. Of course, problems remain, and backsliding is a possibility. Police sometimes take detainees to vacant lots or outside the city limits, provoking fears that they may shift to the "L.A. Confidential" system—after the film of the same name—of torturing detainees in a "safe house" or unregistered detention center.

"For decades, documenting torture in Turkey was extremely discouraging work. But the fact that Turkey has turned the corner on torture means that it can happen elsewhere," said Jeri Laber.

Given the distinct improvement, it is worth examining how Turkey has managed to curb torture: First, simply spotlighting a country's torture practices can help create domestic and diplomatic pressure to stop torture. Second, access to prisons and police stations by independent investigators is vital. Not knowing when an inspection may happen keeps police who might otherwise be tempted to get a confession the "easy" way off balance, and they may give a second thought before torturing. Third, shortening detention periods, and finally, abolishing incommunicado detention and ensuring immediate access to legal counsel in police stations can make a big difference. Turkey now has excellent protections against torture in law, but supervision of police stations is still poor, which is why ill-treatment is still being reported.

The "struggle against terror" has been used routinely by the Turkish authorities to excuse torture. Turkey has had a long-standing problem with political violence and armed opposition groups, on a much larger scale than in other European countries. Turkey still has armed and violent insurgents. Despite this, now that the technical steps have been taken to open up the closed world of the interrogation center, torture is on the wane.

Where torture is currently the worst in the world today is where it is most cost-free for the perpetrators. If Turkey can turn the corner on torture, then progress should be possible in the rest of the world. In fact, with some alterations for local situations, the model of how the tide is being turned in Turkey could work in Uzbekistan, China, Egypt, Uganda, and Brazil as well.

"I hear talk about attacking the culture of torture through education, but I don't believe there is a cultural propensity to torture in Turkey or anywhere else. This is a question of political will to apply technical measures," said Sugden. "Even in a country where there are still illegal armed groups and violent clashes, as soon as the Turkish authorities applied the standard remedies against torture, it began to fade away."

8

ON NEGOTIATING WITH TORTURERS

Sir Nigel Rodley, interviewed by Amy D. Bernstein

One of the world's leading authorities on the law of torture, Sir Nigel Rodley is a long-standing professor of law at the University of Essex and the head of its Human Rights Centre. Professor Rodley was the United Nations' Special Rapporteur on Torture from 1993 to 2001, during which time he investigated allegations of torture worldwide. He is currently an Expert Member of the UN Human Rights Committee and a commissioner of the International Commission of Jurists. He offers here an account of confronting torturing governments and trying to convince them to change their behavior. This piece draws from interviews held with Amy D. Bernstein in November 2004.

The position of Special Rapporteur on Torture was created in 1985 and was potentially very open-ended. It was created to assess information, usually from nongovernmental organizations, about the incidence of torture around the world. In cases where people had been detained and were at risk of torture, an urgent appeal would be faxed to the foreign ministry of the government in question, and another copy sent to its permanent delegation at the UN. In cases where torture was documented, we would send a letter to the country, usually through its permanent delegation in Geneva, with a summary of individual allegations, as well as descriptions of possible wider practices and legal context that had been brought to the UN's attention. In addition, we might seek to visit a particular country where there seemed to be a more extensive practice of torture. The UN Special Rapporteur on Torture doesn't have an automatic right to visit—countries can choose to extend an invitation or not. If invited, the Special Rapporteur does a field mission to find out what the obstacles are to implementing the country's anti-torture law, because torture is prohibited in the laws of most countries—and then we would make recommendations. In the end, there is no coercive power there. It's only the power of persuasion, prodding, and peer pressure.

I went to some fourteen countries as Special Rapporteur on Torture, and access to detainees was a condition of my visiting any country. We developed standard terms of reference for fact-finding missions, the same as those used by the UN Commission on Human Rights. They require states to make available senior officials, as well as officials at other levels. They allowed us access to any place of detention that we chose, whenever we chose, and to talk to whomever we chose inside or outside the place of detention. It was modeled in many ways on the practice of the International Committee of the Red Cross (ICRC). In a few instances, I was denied access to specific sites during a mission. For instance, during a mission to Kenya, I was supposed to go to the main prison in Nairobi, and I was denied access. That was a straight, flagrant denial of promised cooperation—it was on the agreed schedule. Possibly it was a kind of punishment—earlier, I had visited another prison in another town where I had been able to discover that they had substantially reduced the population of the prison before I got there. A lot of those people had been transferred to the Nairobi prison. So they might have decided that there was just stuff that they didn't want me to see or hear in the Nairobi prison. As the visit was to take place on my last day in the country, I couldn't credibly threaten to abandon the mission if I couldn't secure access. But most of the time there was cooperation from almost everybody.

I did not seek to visit countries that already had their own country-specific rapporteur. These were countries that were unpopular enough that they couldn't prevent the votes in the UN Commission on Human Rights to establish a rapporteur on them. As a result, a country-specific rapporteur is often seen as the UN nuclear weapon, so much so that sometimes countries can end up agreeing to something even more intrusive to avoid that fate. A good example of this was Colombia, where I undertook a joint mission with the Special Rapporteur on Summary and Arbitrary Executions. In a meeting with their army high command, you had generals who had barely heard of the UN, saying, "The one thing we don't want is a [country-specific] special rapporteur on us." A couple of years after our mission and our report, it was possible for a UN human rights office to be set up in Bogotá, with power to intervene with any authorities, to meet with NGOs, and to investigate virtually any allegations, so it was by far the most intrusive mechanism available. Our other conditions were agreed to for fear that a country-specific rapporteur—who would only be able to parachute into the country once or twice a year—would be appointed.

China offers a very interesting example of the process of negotiating a mission with a country's authorities. They invited me to visit in 1999, so when I was in Geneva, I met with Chinese officials to review the standard terms of reference for fact-finding visits of the Commission on Human Rights. After a quick look, they said, "Oh, we haven't invited you for a fact-finding visit, we've invited you for a friendly visit," and suggested we should cooperate to work things out on the ground. But I wasn't prepared to play that kind of game. It was hard enough to do a proper mission under the standard operating terms. So there was a virtual standoff for a couple of years, in which they kept saying they'd invited me, and I kept saying they hadn't invited me for what I had asked for. After I resigned, I think they were a bit surprised that my successor, Theo van Boven, stuck to my guns. Eventually, they invited him on the standard terms, but then postponed the invitation indefinitely. Regrettably, some other UN mechanisms, such as the Working Group on Arbitrary Detention, had been willing to negotiate on the ground. They argued that just being there was probably a contribution and were able to point to some kinds of valuable access they had been given. I think they made a serious mistake. At the time, there was a lot of concern expressed at the way they had dealt with China. But I'm sure they did it with the best will in the world.

Upon arrival, one is usually met by a delegation from the country's Foreign Ministry. Meetings with government ministers and other officials, senior and not so senior, are followed by visits to prisons, and more important, unannounced visits to police stations. With that process, one is able to dig up quite a lot of information. If one goes to a country like Brazil, like Cameroon, not particularly experienced in dealing with this kind of visit, you can still fall over the evidence, frankly. When you talk directly to the prisoners, they tell you where the bars they were beaten with are located. You go to where they say, and there they are. There is no way they could know unless their story is true. You see the ribbons and scars on their bodies. You don't have to be a medical practitioner to form a reasonable assessment of the truth.

Anyhow, one of the things that the mission doesn't try to do is establish the truth of every individual allegation. Rather, we're looking at the pattern. I would talk to different people in different institutions, or different people in different parts of the same institution, who didn't know I was going to be there and certainly didn't have a chance to get their stories together. They would all name the same torturer, and I could see that there was a problem. In the case of Cameroon, it was clear, as we went from one police station to another, that they hadn't had visits of this sort before. They hadn't done any kind of cleanup operation, or emptied out any of their places of detention in any of the areas we were likely to visit. Sometimes, there was amazing candor. In one prison in Cameroon, we were being shown around by the director. Most of the cells were pretty crowded, and we went into one dark cell, and there were two naked men. The director said that these two people had just been arrested on suspicion of having killed a policeman. They were not in good shape and we asked for an explanation. Already he was embarrassed by what we had seen. He said, "You can see this has been an open tour, because I could have made sure you didn't come across such things." We talked about his problems in imposing discipline on his own guards. We heard stories of some of his people victimizing inmates, and he said that sometimes inmates have done nasty things to the guards. He also referred to one particular case where he himself had administered a beating to a prisoner to prevent his guards from doing something worse. It was a very interesting kind of candor, showing a clear weakness in the system. One always assumes that in a hierarchy, the people higher up control the people lower down. That's not always the case.

One also always tends to think of the torture issue as torture of politicals, and that's how it came onto the international agenda, back in the early seventies. But by the time I was doing the job, there were far fewer politicals. I was looking more and more at ordinary common-criminal suspects, usually people at the pretrial stage, and in many countries, *it was really bad*. One doesn't even know whether it's always been like that, or that we've only just started to look at common criminals, or whether periods of repressive habits have finally started to spill over into the criminal justice system. The classic purposes of torture are to get information or confessions. And the information can be in respect of the person's own suspected guilt, or in relation to somebody else's activities, as part of an investigative process. In some prisons, it may be for disciplining purposes as well.

There were only two times when I had really serious obstacles put in the way of my access to prisoners. One was on my second mission, to Russia, where I first came across the rule that pertained throughout the ex-Soviet sphere, that unconvicted, detained suspects were not allowed to talk unsupervised to outsiders without the okay of the investigator or prosecutor. It was partly as a result of that lesson that I moved for systematization of the operative rules so that when I went a few years later to Azerbaijan, and met the same argument, I said, "Look, these are the terms of reference you agreed to; I expect compliance," and they complied. The ICRC had also been trying to negotiate an agreement with Azerbaijan to have access to prisoners. It was precisely this prohibition of unsupervised access to prisoners in pretrial detention that was preventing their deal. All of a sudden, I walk in for ten days, and break straight through the rule. At that point it was very hard for them to maintain to the ICRC that this rule was absolute and unbreakable. Within a matter of weeks the ICRC too got its agreement.

The second instance of noncompliance was the incident in Kenya, which I mentioned earlier.

Russia was an unusual mission because they had invited me unsolicited in 1994. We hadn't had any entries on them for the previous year or two, so I didn't even know what I was supposed to be looking at. It only became clear as we came closer to the mission that some people who were former prisoners of conscience and were now in the relevant unit of the Foreign Ministry wanted the Ministry of the Interior to clean up its act, especially in the area of prison conditions. Except for maybe some police lockups in Brazil, I had never seen anything of the sort I saw in Russian pretrial detention centers, mainly in Moscow but also in St. Petersburg. In the "general cells" of two detention centers in Moscow, where there was room for about thirty people at a pinch, there were some 90 to 120 people. It was repulsive. You opened the door and what issued was indescribable. I said in my report that you would have to have the painterly skills of a Bosch or the poetic skills of a Dante to describe the reality inside. I suddenly understood that behind this word "overcrowding" you could have something that was infernal and absolutely shocking.

It made me think again about the definition of torture, which in addition to the imposition of severe pain or suffering requires a purpose, such as obtaining information or a confession. What I found myself doing was describing these conditions as "torturous," but I couldn't say they constituted torture because I didn't have the evidence that they were being used for one of those very narrow purposes. But I suspected that prosecutors and investigators got suspects banged up in there in order to get them to cooperate. It was pretty disturbing stuff, and my report got a fair amount of attention. It may even have had something to do with why the Council of Europe put very heavy pressure on Russia to clean up its act before allowing it to become a member, and why Russia agreed to become a party to the European Convention for the Prevention of Torture, which requires states to accept periodic and sometimes ad hoc inspections in any place of detention. The European Committee for the Prevention of Torture, operating under that Convention, has done some important follow-up work to my own, and I believe that the kind of conditions I described are not so prevalent now.

When, as is usually the case, governments deny the use of torture, you talk to the authorities and ask them a lot of questions about what they do when they get information alleging torture, what they have done in each case, and take them through it. It sometimes involves, when you know that a particular prisoner has had a rough time, asking to see them, and if you're told that the prisoner has been moved, finding out where they've been moved to. It happened in Kenya. It happened in Brazil. We've had to do some tracking from institution to institution to find some people who were in pretty bad shape, and get them some medical attention. That's a process of confrontation. It is also a process of elucidating the facts.

The classic situation of torture is the authoritarian, unconstitutional military government repressing opposition of any kind, peaceful or otherwise, by whatever terroristic means they deem appropriate, but in most countries it's not like that, thank goodness. There has been an improvement—in that sense—in the world. Sometimes where torture is practiced, the governments are just turning a blind eye. Sometimes, they might also be told by their militaries, Okay, we're going to deal with this armed opposition, but you've got to cover for us. But sometimes, I genuinely think that people may not know, or they are trying hard not to know. In Kenya, for example, after we had been thrown out of a police station, we were accompanied by an assistant commissioner of police for a good chunk of the mission. We had complained to the chief commissioner of police and his assistant commissioner had been assigned to us. A few days later we went back unannounced to that very same police station and got some more useful information. I got the impression that by the end of the mission the assistant commissioner was shocked at some of the abuses we uncovered. I'm certain that to get to his level he couldn't have been totally ignorant of police practice, but at the same time he did seem genuinely surprised. The reason I went to Kenya, of course, was because there had been substantial allegations of torture. We didn't seek to go to countries where it was just the occasional, isolated case. Yet did it seem like one of the worst countries in the world? No. But usually, what one gets from the nongovernmental organizations' reporting is often the tip of a really big iceberg.

Generally speaking, governments don't seek to justify torture directly. They *can't,* because they are then admitting to something that is a violation of their own laws, not just international law. In the mission to Colombia, I was taken by the minister of Defense to the meeting of the Armed Forces High Command. The minister of Defense took the view publicly and certainly with us that there was a systematic problem of torture and extrajudicial killings and disappearances, yet at the meeting of the High Command, every single one of the army officers insisted that there were only isolated instances, because they knew that that had to be the formal position, and of course their necks were much more on the block than the minister's. It is very rare for anybody to admit as much as this minister of Defense did. More usually there would be similar kinds of circumlocutions of the sort that the Turks noted: "No, we don't do it, but our police are not well enough trained." "No, we don't do it, but our police don't know how to interrogate properly." So, on the one hand they say they don't do it, on the other they are giving reasons why it may be happening. Similarly, I have been to places where some of the warders are trying to hide stuff, but some of the social-services staff are trying to put you on the right track, because they are not too happy with what is going on.

I have always felt a little sorry in retrospect for the director of the central jail in Lahore, in Pakistan. I had made clear to the Interior minister that one of the things I would consider as a success criterion for that mission was if something were done about prison use of bar fetters—shackles around the feet with a chain and a bar attached to a metal hoop around the waist, so prisoners couldn't stretch out their feet entirely and had to hobble everywhere. Very nasty stuff. He pointed out that the British had introduced the system in regulations drawn up in the nineteenth century. I told him, "Well, next year is the fiftieth anniversary of your independence; wouldn't that be a nice time to get rid of this particular colonial legacy?" I had been told that these bar fetters were a feature in every prison, but I found none in Lahore Central Jail, the first prison I went to. When asked, the prison officials said, "Oh, we only use them for transferring detainees from prison to court, as a security measure." While touring the prison, I talked in confidence to some prisoners, and they said 200 or 300 sets had been removed the previous night. When we got to the windup meeting in the director's office, I asked for the fetters log provided for in the regulations, and they brought it. Going back months and months, there were people who had been fettered for all sorts of reasons. The records showed there were still some that hadn't been removed after eight months or more. I asked for the information on this, and they admitted, "Well, we removed them last night." Occasionally you can simply confront them with their own information. But that doesn't happen all the time.

We could speculate for hours on why governments behave the way they do, starting with why they have developed an international law of human rights, which is basically a stick to beat themselves with—if that's not an inappropriate metaphor. They have to make the calculation as to which is going to cause the greater opprobrium—to invite or not to invite a UN special rapporteur. They must also calculate whether they will be able to hide enough, and how to react afterward. I have had governments react ferociously and I have had governments react very positively. There isn't an automatic correlation between how tough a torture report is and how harsh or positive the reaction is. Probably the hardest report I have ever written was my last report, on Brazil, in 2000, where, once the press got hold of my methods of operation, they started following me around, and I was being filmed on television as I was finding instruments of torture. It was bizarre. They just said, "We're going to launch a national campaign to try and do something about this." The media thanked me for the work.

In terms of follow-up, the first step is the report, which contains a long list of recommendations. But then we would try to implement a rudimentary follow-up to that, by which basically once a year, we would ask each country to report on what it had done in respect to each of our recommendations, and in the annual report we would include in the entry on that country their responses. It was not exactly the most intrusive follow-up, but at least it kept the issues alive. I would occasionally learn from nongovernmental sources that interdepartmental working groups were moving forward on some of these recommendations, and the governments hadn't even bothered to inform us. . . . All one can do at the UN level in this field is to keep it at the level of dialogue in the public domain. That is an achievement of the last quarter-century. Before that, it wasn't remotely possible.

9

SEXUAL VIOLENCE, TORTURE, AND INTERNATIONAL JUSTICE

Cherie Booth

Cherie Booth is a Fellow of the International Society of Lawyers for Public Service, where she works on issues such as children's rights, the rights of women, the international judiciary, and the influence of international law in domestic courts. Her piece examines sexual violence and torture of women around the world, particularly in armed conflicts such as the recent Darfur crisis, and looks at recent jurisprudential advances in prosecuting those who torture by rape.

Max du Plessis, Associate Professor, Faculty of Law, University of KwaZulu-Natal, Durban, and Advocate of the High Court of South Africa, also contributed to this essay.

Mwanvua has just told a lie and everyone in the room knows it. She stares at her feet, silent. The 14-year-old is back home after months as the prisoner of vagabond soldiers, relating her ordeal.

It is the obvious question, and her family ask it: how many of her 13 kidnappers raped her? In little more than a whisper, Mwanvua replies "one."

Her parents and siblings exchange looks but say nothing. Nobody believes her. Not taking her eyes off the earth floor, after some minutes Mwanvua speaks again, the voice firmer this time. "All of them. They all passed through me." [1]

It is a tragic fact of life that appalling numbers of sex crimes are perpetrated against women civilians around the world, in an age-old but increasingly prevalent form of torture. Amnesty International records that at least 40,000 female civilians, girls and women, have been raped over the last six years in the Congo alone.[2] A recent Human Rights Watch report on the legacy of mass rape in the Democratic Republic of Congo[3] chronicles the level of violence against women in that country, the role that rape and other forms of sexual horror play in the perpetration of that violence, and the almost absolute levels of impunity that follow such crimes. In recent years, sexual torture of this kind has been documented in Rwanda, the Sudan, Yugoslavia, Iraq, and East Timor, among other countries.

A look at Yugoslavia makes vividly clear the role of sexual violence and rape as a tool of war. During the Balkan crisis, women became the hapless victims of marauding soldiers bent on murder and rape. One particular atrocity involved a systematic Serb policy of the repeated rape of Bosnian Muslim women until pregnant and then forcibly detaining these women until they delivered children—all in order to "cleanse" the ethnic composition of the children.[4] Rape as a form of torture was also a common occurrence.

Instances of rape as torture during the reign of Saddam Hussein are slowly emerging in reports on Iraq. Although there has largely been a deafening silence about the use of rape as a weapon of war in a Muslim society where it is such an enormous disgrace for a woman to be violated, it is clear that many women were raped in Iraq. An index card for a man who had a secret contact with the general security organization, file number 43,304, identified his activity as "violation of women's honor." Rape has been used to crush the spirit of political prisoners, to recruit women into the internal spy network, and to "break the eyes" of families and communities.[5]

The horrors of rape are also emerging before the Truth Commission currently established in East Timor.[6] Women described their experiences during the 1980s, as the Indonesian military established its apparatus at the village level. The story of Olga da Silva Amaral is typical: She described before the Commission how women were detained at the Dare Military Command Post and repeatedly raped by Indonesian soldiers. The military put up a building they called a school to hold the women whose husbands had been exiled. The women were ordered to live with the soldiers. Olga told of how she was kept in a toilet for three months, where the torture and sexual abuse continued: "There was never a day without rape." She was released in April 1983 and reunited with her husband, who returned from exile later that year.[7]

The exposure of Rwandan women to sexual violence during and after the genocide in 1994 is well known and has been carefully documented by Human Rights Watch in its report, "Shattered Lives: Sexual Violence during the Rwandan Genocide and its Aftermath."[8] It is estimated that 25,000 women were raped, many of them by HIV-positive men and in circumstances that often amounted to sexual violence as torture. As Mary Kayitesi Blewitt, director of the UK–based Survivors Fund (SURF), records, women have testified that rapes occurred after they had been forced to watch their families cut down: "You alone are being allowed to live," the soldiers would taunt, "so that you will die of sadness."[9] The stories these survivors share are moving and painful. One young woman described how she was raped by ten or more men in the presence of her two-year-old child. She was later attacked by two other men who raped her but didn't bother to remove the child that was strapped to her back. Fortunately, the child survived. The mother is currently struggling tremendously with pain in her uterus, and has tested positive for HIV. Her words are haunting: "Right now, when I think about it, I want to kill myself and die. . . . My suffering isn't visible, like it is with people who have very noticeable scars or who have had limbs chopped off. But my wound is there, inside."

The Sudanese crisis is of course a latter-day tragedy involving similarly galling accounts of violence against women. The recent UN

Commission's 176-page report documents a series of crimes against humanity, including women and girls being kept naked in rape camps.[10]

These recent stories of appalling sexual violence against women are unfortunately modern repeats of an age-old nightmare. In the arena of armed conflict, history is replete with examples of women being targeted as victims of sexual torture. Rape and other acts of sexual violence have long been utilized as instruments of warfare, used not only as an attack on the individual victim but also as a means to "humiliate, shame, degrade and terrify the entire . . . group."[11] Victims have been let down when it has come to the prevention and prosecution of these offenses, largely because sexual violence has been regarded as an accepted concomitant of war, even if it was not explicitly condoned. General Patton's writings about the Second World War in his book titled *War as I Knew It* reflect the "inevitability" of rape in times of war. Patton remembers that in spite of his most diligent efforts, "there would unquestionably be some raping," and that he demanded the details as early as possible so that the offenders could be appropriately dealt with.[12]

Besides the *inevitability* of sexual violence, rape has historically served a tactical function in war as an expression of the totality of victory—a sort of sexual coup de grace. The story is told of the Byzantine emperor Alexius, who, in appealing for recruits during the First Crusade, extolled the beauty of Greek women as an incentive to go to war, an idea which later came to be known as that of "booty and beauty," and which was associated with success in battle. As the events in Rwanda and the former Yugoslavia so horribly remind us, this function of sexual aggression against women often serves as a grotesque public display of domination where the "rape of the woman's body symbolically represents the rape of the community itself."[13] At the international level it was only in relatively recent times that sexual violence against women during armed conflict came to be regarded as an important issue in serious need of redress.

One way in which women came to receive justice was by means of the ad hoc International Criminal Tribunals established in the wake of mass atrocities in the former Yugoslavia and Rwanda. For example, the celebrated Akayesu case, the first heard before the International Criminal Tribunal for Rwanda and heralded today as possibly "the most important decision rendered thus far in the history of women's jurisprudence,"[14] was not only the first international war crimes trial in history to try and convict a defendant for genocide, but also the first judgment in which an accused has been found guilty of genocide for crimes that expressly included sexualized violence and the first time that an accused has been found guilty of rape as a crime against humanity.

Judge Navanethem Pillay, a South African Indian and the only female judge on the Rwandan tribunal at the time, presided over the February 1997 trial. Surprisingly, given what we now know of the Rwandan situation, no charges or evidence of rape were initially brought at the trial, with the prosecutor claiming that it was impossible to document rape because women would not talk about it.[15] However, Judge Pillay delicately pursued a line of inquiry with two women—called by the prosecutor to testify to *other* crimes—as to whether rape had occurred in the Commune. The first witness explained how she had fled her village before the slaughter began and had managed to hide in a tree, where she stayed for several days. After deciding it was safe, she climbed down to discover that only her six-year-old daughter had survived a massacre in which the rest of her family was killed. Together they tried to escape the area but were caught by Hutus who gang-raped her daughter.

Her sworn statement taken before the trial mirrored this evidence given in court about the murders but was silent about the details of her daughter's rape, apparently because the investigators had not asked her about rape. After further careful examination by Judge Pillay, the witness also testified that she had heard that young girls were raped at the Taba

Commune where Jean-Paul Akayesu was in charge. The second witness confirmed this. She testified that she had been taken into custody and held at the bureau, where Akayesu had stood and watched as girls were dragged into the compound and repeatedly raped by armed militia. Commenting on this situation, Judge Pillay said:

> We have to try a case before us where this person [Akayesu] has not been specifically charged with rape. We're hearing the evidence, but the defense counsel has not cross-examined the witnesses who gave testimony of sexual violence, because it is not in the indictment. I'm extremely dismayed that we're hearing evidence of rape and sexual violence against women and children, yet it is not in the indictments because the witnesses were never asked about it.[16]

The consequence was that in June 1997 the indictment was amended by the prosecutor to add charges of sexual violence. When the trial resumed, extensive testimony concerning rape and other forms of sexual violence was admitted into evidence—evidence that was used to establish that sexual violence was an integral part of the genocide committed during the Rwandan conflict.[17]

As the jurisprudence of the Yugoslavia and Rwanda tribunals developed, rape came to be associated with torture.[18] The severe mental and physical pain and suffering caused by rape and sexual assault led the trial chambers of both ad hoc tribunals to hold that rape and sexual assault can constitute torture. In the Akayesu case, the Rwanda trial chamber drew upon the Torture Convention[19] to draw comparisons between torture and rape, holding that:

> Like torture, rape is used for such purposes as intimidation, degradation, humiliation, discrimination, punishment, control or destruction of a person. Like torture, rape is a violation of personal dignity, and rape in fact

constitutes torture when inflicted by or at the instigation of or with the consent or acquiescence of a public official or other person acting in an official capacity.[20]

The same thinking has informed the jurisprudence of the International Criminal Tribunal for the former Yugoslavia. For example, in the notorious Celebici case[21] the ICTY dealt with atrocities committed in early May 1992 when Bosnian Muslims and Croats took control of Bosnian Serb villages in the Konjic municipality. Men and women were taken to a facility that came to be known as the Celebici camp. Aside from other atrocities committed, the deputy commander of the camp, Hazim Delic, was indicted by the Yugoslav Tribunal for having tortured by way of rape two Serb female prisoners. The Tribunal found that: "Rape causes severe pain and suffering, both physical and psychological. The psychological suffering of persons upon whom rape is inflicted may be exacerbated by social and cultural conditions and can be particularly acute and long lasting." In addition, it commented that "it is difficult to envisage circumstances in which rape, by, or at the instigation of a public official, or with the consent or acquiescence of an official, could be considered as occurring for a purpose that does not, in some way, involve punishment, coercion, discrimination or intimidation." In the Tribunal's view, this purpose, which is classically associated with the crime of torture, "is inherent in situations of armed conflict."[22]

In respect to the first victim, for instance, Delic was found guilty of torture by rape inasmuch as he committed the rapes "to obtain information about the whereabouts of [the victim's] husband who was considered an armed rebel; to punish her for her inability to provide information about her husband; to coerce or intimidate her into providing such information; and to punish her for the acts of her husband."[23] In addition, the violence suffered by the victim in the form of rape was inflicted upon her by Delic because she is a woman. To the

Tribunal, "this represents a form of discrimination which constitutes a prohibited purpose for the offence of torture."[24]

A prosecutorial response to such alarming sexual violence is vital if any semblance of justice is to be done. More and more victims are keen to take their cases to court. According to a counselor interviewed by Human Rights Watch who works with victims of sexual violence:

> Many women I speak to want to take their case to justice. They say, "I wish he would be punished today." When you explain to them that they can conceal their identity in court, they say: "I have nothing to lose. I am ready to stand in court and say openly what happened."[25]

For the victims of sexual violence, the last decade or so has ushered in the possibility of prosecution of offenders under international criminal law. Since 1990 this specialized body of criminal law has made greater progress on women's issues than during any other time in recorded history. The most important milestone in relation to the prosecution of sexual violence, including sexual violence as torture, has been the creation of a permanent International Criminal Court. The Statute of the International Criminal Court was adopted on July 17, 1998, by an overwhelming majority of the states attending the Rome Conference, a conference specifically organized to secure agreement on a treaty for the establishment of a permanent international criminal tribunal. The ICC Statute entered into force on July 1, 2002, at which time the Court's jurisdiction over genocide, war crimes, and crimes against humanity took effect. The ICC Statute puts in place individual criminal liability for those responsible for the most serious human rights violations, and creates a permanent institution to ensure the punishment of such criminals. The Court's first case will in all likelihood be either a prosecution of Ugandan rebel leaders of the Lord's Resistance

Army who have kidnapped thousands of children and forced them to serve as soldiers or sex slaves,[26] or the targeting of recent crimes committed in the territory of the DRC.[27]

The Court's aim is to be a truly international criminal tribunal, but its jurisdiction is limited to the states that choose to become party to its statute. The Court will only have jurisdiction over those offenses committed on the territory of a state that is party to the ICC Statute, and over the nationals of state parties that commit ICC offenses. To date, the ICC Statute has been signed by 139 states, and 97 states have ratified it.[28] Of those 97 states, 26 are African—a not insignificant proportion. The DRC government has opted to ratify the statute of the ICC, which is particularly important for victims in the DRC. And for the child sex-slaves in Uganda, there is hope inasmuch as their state has chosen to become a party to the ICC regime as well. Both countries, faced with unruly bands of soldiers or resistance movements that are beyond the government's capability to prosecute, have relied on a provision in the ICC Statute that allows them to refer cases for investigation to the Court where they are unable to do so themselves. While Sudan is not a party to the ICC Statute, the UN Security Council, using its powers under Chapter VII of the United Nations Charter, referred the "situation" in Sudan to the International Criminal Court for investigation.[29] The findings of the special United Nations commission, led by the Italian judge Antonio Cassese, which had been investigating violence in the Darfur region in western Sudan, has found that the violence, including sexual violence, amounted to "crimes against humanity with ethnic dimensions."

For those criminals over which the ICC has jurisdiction, sexual exploitation and violence against women—such as that directed against Mwanvua by her thirteen kidnappers in the DRC—could feature high on the list of cases the Court will be investigating. These cases arise from a continent that is home to many of the international human rights atrocities, both past and continuing, which haunt humanity in what appears to be repeating cycles.

For victims of sexual violence, the ICC Statute that established the Court both exemplifies the progress thus far and hints at the future contribution that institutions such as the newly formed International Criminal Court can make to the attainment of justice for women. For one thing, the Statute allows for prosecution of a wide range of sex-based crimes. Aside from prohibiting sexual violence as a war crime in Article 8, Article 7(2)(g) of the ICC Statute specifically proscribes the crime against humanity constituted by "rape; sexual slavery; enforced prostitution; forced pregnancy; enforced sterilization; or any other form of sexual violence of comparable gravity."

Due to the important work done by the ad hoc tribunals for Rwanda and Yugoslavia, a rapidly developing jurisprudence has arisen around crimes of sexual violence. The International Criminal Tribunal for Rwanda has spelled out the broad parameters of the crime of rape by stating that it involves "a physical invasion of a sexual nature, committed under circumstances that are coercive; it may or may not involve sexual intercourse."[30] The Elements of Crimes in the ICC Statute sets out its own (broadly similar) requirements in the case of rape. In terms of the Elements of Crimes, rape that amounts to a crime against humanity occurs where:

1) The perpetrator invaded the body of a person by conduct resulting in penetration, however slight, of any part of the body of the victim or of the perpetrator with a sexual organ, or of the anal or genital opening of the victim with any object or any other part of the body.

2) The invasion was committed by force, or by threat of force or coercion, such as that caused by fear of violence, duress, detention, psychological oppression or abuse of power, against such person or

another person, or by taking advantage of a coercive environment, or the invasion was committed against a person incapable of giving genuine consent (because of natural, induced, or age-related incapacity).

3) The conduct was committed as part of a widespread or systematic attack directed against a civilian population.

4) The perpetrator knew that the conduct was part of or intended the conduct to be part of a widespread or systematic attack directed against a civilian population.

In the context of sexual slavery—a disturbingly prevalent crime in the DRC and Uganda—there may be an overlap with the crime against humanity of enslavement. According to the ICC Statute, enslavement "means the exercise of any or all of the powers attaching to the right of ownership over a person and includes the exercise of such power in the course of trafficking in persons, in particular women and children."[31] The elements of this crime are best set out in the ICTY Trial Chamber's decision in Kunarac and others,[32] where the Tribunal held that indications of enslavement include:

- elements of control and ownership
- the restriction or control of an individual's autonomy, freedom of choice or freedom of movement (often with the accruing of some gain to the perpetrator)
- the absence of consent or free will on the part of the victim (usually rendered impossible or irrelevant by, for example, fear of violence, deception or false promises, abuse of power, the victim's position of vulnerability, detention or captivity, psychological oppression or socio-economic conditions)

Along with these indicators of enslavement are exploitation, sex, prostitution, and human trafficking.

Torture as a crime against humanity has been given a broad definition under the ICC Statute.[33] For the purposes of the crime against humanity of torture, the perpetrator must have inflicted severe physical or
mental pain or suffering upon one or more persons who were in the
perpetrator's custody or under his control. Such pain or suffering must
have been committed as part of a widespread or systematic attack directed against a civilian population, and the perpetrator must have
known or intended that the conduct was part of such an attack. No specific purpose need be proved for the crime of torture as a crime against
humanity.[34]

What is clear from the preceding discussion is that a broad range of
sexually violent acts against women has come to be prohibited under
the Statute of the International Criminal Court. These acts singly or in
combination may in addition amount to torture, either as a crime
against humanity insofar as the pain or suffering is inflicted as part of a
widespread or systematic attack directed against the civilian population,
or as a war crime insofar as the sexual attack is inflicted during a time of
international armed conflict for one of the traditional purposes of torture—namely, extracting information or a confession, punishment, intimidation or coercion, or in order to discriminate.

The prosecutor of the International Criminal Court (drawing inspiration from decisions such as those of the ad hoc tribunals in the
Akayesu and Celebici cases) will thus in appropriate circumstances be
able to charge offenders who have committed egregious sexual acts
against women with the cumulative offenses of torture as a crime
against humanity or war crime, and rape or other sexual violence such
as enslavement and sexual slavery prohibited under the ICC Statute.[35]

While the DRC, Uganda, and the Sudan are currently in the ICC's
spotlight, Africa is not alone in harboring the rapists, killers, and thugs
who are worthy of attention under the International Criminal Court's
regime. For women, the crime of sexual violence knows no bound-

aries—no continent provides women safe sanctuary from the predatory behavior of rapists.

The victims of rape as a war crime or crime against humanity live with the consequences for the rest of their lives. As if the torturous violence and its physical and psychological aftermath were not enough, victims suffer other horrors such as rape-related HIV/AIDS. There is a need to ensure that justice is served for this most vulnerable group of women survivors by enabling these women to lead active lives again by giving them critical access to antiretroviral treatment. We would suggest that the international community has a general obligation to secure antiretroviral treatment for the thousands of women survivors raped and deliberately infected with HIV. Otherwise we could be faced with the terrible irony in places like Rwanda—that the perpetrators of rape receive the necessary drugs in prison whilst awaiting trial before the ICTR, and their hapless victims, infected by them with HIV/AIDS, are dying untreated outside the prisons before they can be called to give their evidence.

Aside from enabling women survivors to maintain a meaningful existence after sexual violence, justice might be served by prosecuting those who torture by rape. Building on the jurisprudential advances of the ad hoc tribunals for Rwanda and Yugoslavia, such prosecution can now take place before the newly created International Criminal Court, a court that is intended to operate across boundaries, with potential jurisdiction to prosecute offenders wherever they might be found. While one leading commentator in the field rightly reminds us that "it is important to be modest about the potential of war crimes trials and international criminal law generally,"[36] modesty or realism when it comes to the International Criminal Court need not be cynicism. The Court, with independent prosecutors putting killers, torturers, and rapists in the dock before independent judges, is a signal—a warning, if you will—that state parties will not tolerate the violence and torture, sexual or otherwise, that threatens our humanity. For the many thousands of women who are the subjects of torturous sexual violence, the Court will therefore stand as a beacon of hope. The decision in April 2005 by the UN Security Council to refer the case of Darfur to the ICC is of historic importance. Among the many terrible crimes committed in Darfur, the referral paves the way for the prosecution of widespread rapes by the Janjaweed militias against civilians there. It remains for the judges, the prosecutor, the NGO community, and states committed to the ICC to ensure that the Court becomes not merely a symbolic beacon of hope but an effective tool in the investigation and prosecution of the unique form of torture represented by sexual violence against women.

10

TREATING TORTURE VICTIMS

Dr. Mary R. Fabri

Dr. Mary R. Fabri is the director of the Marjorie Kovler Center for the Treatment of Survivors of Torture at the Heartland Alliance for Human Needs and Human Rights. She has treated survivors of torture, trained therapists, and consulted nationally and internationally on the issues and methods related to treatment of torture survivors. In this essay, she describes the devastating long-term effects of torture and some of the strategies used to treat those who have suffered this modern-day scourge.

Other essays in this book have discussed whether in any circumstances a society is justified in using torture as a means of extracting information or a confession. From the perspective of a clinical psychologist, the physical and psychological damage to human beings resulting from torture is often so devastating, with such a profound impact, that it cannot be viewed as an acceptable practice in any scenario. Recovery from the serious trauma resulting from torture can be a long and arduous path, fraught with lifelong vulnerabilities. The destructive effect of torture on the human psyche and physique also undermines the moral fiber of a society—which must bear responsibility for what it has purposely inflicted on its fellow human beings.

I have chosen three case histories to illustrate a medical perspective on torture and the work that I have done, for nearly two decades now, with torture survivors, first as a volunteer and now as director of the Marjorie Kovler Center for the Treatment of Survivors of Torture at the

Heartland Alliance. Each survivor's story is unique, and their countries of origin are distinct, but the painful recoveries of these people share some particularities. Most observable is the dignity and strength of each one who has managed to survive the unthinkable and who continues to live with the tremendous personal anguish of torture.

For some survivors, everyday life in the United States is filled with reminders of their torture. Elena, a physician, had learned about the condition called posttraumatic stress disorder during her training in Latin America, and had even recognized it in patients she treated before her own abduction and torture. Escaping to the United States and receiving political asylum, Elena agreed to try prescribed medication to alleviate the insomnia, nightmares, uncontrollable weeping, depression, loss of appetite, weight loss, and intrusive thoughts and memories of being raped. With the persistence of the symptoms, she finally agreed to see a therapist at the Marjorie Kovler Center. The anticipation of meeting with a therapist and talking about her torture created more stress. When she saw the psychiatrist, she limited the discussion to her symptoms and did not tell him the details of her traumatic history. In fact, Elena had never told anyone the details of her torture.

When Elena arrived for her first appointment, I met a slight, nervous woman, who seemed tentative about meeting with me. Sitting down, I smiled and asked how she was feeling about coming to see me. Before she could answer, Elena had a flashback, a neuropsychological reaction resulting in a disconnection from awareness of the present, and the re-experiencing of a traumatic event as if it were occurring. Her eyes became glazed and slowly closed as she gripped the arms of the chair. Her body tensed, as she writhed, moaning and saying, "No. No. Stop." It took me by surprise. I sat forward, monitoring her REM-like eye movements, and repeated orienting statements. Eventually, her eyes opened with a startled look, like a deer in headlights. Elena was crying, her nose dripping. She began muttering an apology, saying she wanted to leave. I handed her the box of tissues and uttered comforting words.

Several weeks elapsed before Elena could enter my office without having a flashback. Throughout that time, I continually reassured her that she could choose what she wished to talk about, and that our time together was in a safe place where she could begin to reclaim the strength and integrity torture had tried to destroy. Over time, many aspects of Elena's functioning improved, but flashbacks remained a persistent vulnerability, triggered by sights, sounds, and smells. Recently, Elena declared, "Perhaps I need to stop trying to figure out how to avoid these flashbacks, and learn how to live with them."

Amal, a bright and articulate North African woman, had family ties to an opposition party in her country. The fundamentalist Islamic regime in power arrested her and convicted her of subversive activities. Sentenced to prison, she was tortured, beaten, raped, and subjected to conditions of severe deprivation. Eventually, she escaped prison by means of bribery and fled to the United States, seeking asylum. Through therapy, she began to recover from torture. Learning English easily, she found employment and began a new life. Amal married, but she soon found herself in an abusive relationship and was obliged to seek restraining orders and eventually a divorce. During this time, she became overwhelmed with memories of her imprisonment and torture in her homeland. She was convinced each time she went before a judge that she would be jailed, and she feared deportation. At each court appearance, she needed to have someone there as her link to reality, and to assure her that she would not be unlawfully imprisoned. The sense of safety she had painstakingly built was utterly destroyed. Now she perceives danger everywhere in her daily life, with posttraumatic stress symptoms evident several years after her torture, precipitated by a distressing life event.

•   •   •

Susana, a young, petite, indigenous woman from Central America, presented a particularly difficult challenge for me. After an already devastating childhood, she had been abducted as a young teen, detained, and tortured. Disappeared for more than a year, she was eventually discovered, wandering alone and pregnant. After further harassment and intimidation, including unlawful detentions, she attempted unsuccessfully to cross the U.S.–Mexico border. Finally, a community in the United States sponsored her and sent her to us with the details of her torturous history. Susana had many symptoms of posttraumatic stress. She suffered violent nightmares, during which she would run down the hallway and cower in a corner. She was suspicious of others, and warily vigilant of her surroundings. Under real or perceived stress, Susana could develop an amnesia regarding past traumatic events. This first surfaced when I attempted to create a chronological account of her history in preparation for political asylum proceedings. Susana suggested she write her testimony in between sessions, in a spiral notebook in Spanish. This proceeded as planned for several sessions until without explanation, she missed an appointment. When I finally reached her by phone, Susana responded as if she did not know me, and seemed surprised to hear of her appointments with me. Later, I was able to reach Susana's boyfriend, Carlos. He apologized, saying he should have called me, but something had happened to Susana and he did not know what to do. We arranged an appointment for him to bring her to see me. Susana looked at me strangely, apparently with no memory of our past work together. She agreed to speak with me, with Carlos present. Carlos began by telling us that Susana had been writing in her notebook when he went to bed one night. The next morning she was confused and began asking Carlos questions about herself. Susana remembered waking that morning with no recollection of her personal history. I asked about the notebook, and Carlos gave it to me. Susana recognized her handwriting and I told her what she had been recording in the notebook. Over time, we reconstructed how the overwhelming and painful memories of her traumatic history had produced amnesia. It became evident that Susana was not able to provide a detailed and sequentially organized account of her traumatic history without becoming vulnerable to psychological decompensation. Despite her obvious strength in maintaining successful coping strategies, Susana needed to keep her trauma in separate, disconnected memory "packages."

These examples show how individuals who survive torture can confront short- and long-term consequences, including personality changes. Many survivors describe the psychological effects of torture as a shattering of one's personality, distorting perceptions, altering one's memories and experiences. Torture has profound and persistent consequences, which sometimes inexplicably, violently recur for years after the actual ordeal is over, causing extreme trauma, even years later.

Once, I suggested to a survivor from Guatemala that she should integrate her experience of torture into her personal history. She angrily retorted, "How dare you suggest that I make something so vile a part of myself?"

Yes, I wonder, how dare I ask.

PART II

Torture and the United States

11

BANNED STATE DEPARTMENT PRACTICES

Tom Malinowski

Tom Malinowski is Washington Advocacy Director for Human Rights Watch. Prior to joining Human Rights Watch, he was Special Assistant to President Bill Clinton and, from 1994 to 1998, a speechwriter for Secretaries of State Warren Christopher and Madeleine Albright and a member of the State Department Policy Planning Staff. In this piece he assesses the cost, moral and political, to the United States of practicing the same kinds of torture and abuse it has long condemned abroad. A chart sets out abuses approved by the United States but criticized as torture when used by other countries.

"I stand for 8–12 hours a day. Why is standing limited to four hours?" So read a note scrawled by Secretary of Defense Donald Rumsfeld on a memo outlining interrogation techniques approved for use on prisoners detained at Guantánamo Bay. Rumsfeld was referring to a practice known as "forced standing" in which detainees are simply made to stand motionless for extended periods of time. This was one of a number of interrogation methods, along with sleep deprivation, exposing prisoners to hot and cold temperatures, binding them in painful "stress positions," and stripping them naked, that came to be employed by the United States against terrorist suspects after September 11.

One thing these methods have in common is that they are designed to appear innocuous. We all stand, after all, as Rumsfeld pointed out. We all lose sleep. We all experience discomfort and shame from time to time. But that can't be the same thing as torture. Bloody and gruesome torture is Saddam Hussein having his enemies branded with hot irons, beaten, electrocuted, and raped. Torture is something that dictators do.

As it turns out, however, most of the world's dictators discovered long ago that you can torture a prisoner without leaving visible scars. The deceptively soft methods that some American interrogators employed on Iraqi and Afghan prisoners were perfected in the dungeons of the world's most repressive regimes for precisely that purpose. And had they wanted to know this, all Secretary Rumsfeld and his staff needed to do was to ask their colleagues in the U.S. Department of State.

Each year, the State Department publishes a report on human rights conditions in every country in the world. It is an honest, principled document, mostly unaffected by political and diplomatic considerations. And both before and since the Abu Ghraib scandal, the State Department has condemned as torture some of the very practices that were employed, and for a time officially approved, by the Defense Department.

In its 2003 human rights report, for example, the State Department cites the military dictatorship in Burma for subjecting detainees to "harsh interrogation techniques designed to intimidate and disorient," including forcing them to "squat or assume stressful, uncomfortable, or painful positions for lengthy periods." It states that in Turkey, "because of reduced detention periods, security officials most often used torture methods that did not leave physical traces, including repeated slapping, exposure to cold, stripping and blindfolding, food and sleep deprivation, threats to detainees or family members, dripping water on the head, squeezing of the testicles, and mock executions." The State Department has condemned Pakistan for the use of tight shackling, Saudi Arabia and Iran for sleep deprivation.

Anyone who has worked with torture victims knows that these methods can be as cruel as those involving physical violence. For example, the *Washington Times* reported in 2004 that "[s]ome of the most feared forms of torture cited" by survivors of the North Korean gulag "were surprisingly mundane: Guards would force inmates to stand perfectly still for hours at a time, or make them perform exhausting repetitive exercises such as standing up and sitting down until they collapsed from fatigue." As for sleep deprivation, consider former Israeli prime minister Menachem Begin's account of experiencing it in a Soviet prison in the 1940s:

> In the head of the interrogated prisoner a haze begins to form. His spirit is wearied to death, his legs are unsteady, and he has one sole desire: to sleep, to sleep just a little, not to get up, to lie, to rest, to forget. . . . Anyone who has experienced this desire knows that not even hunger or thirst are comparable with it. . . . I came across prisoners who signed what they were ordered to sign, only to get what the interrogator promised them. He did not promise them their liberty. He promised them—if they signed—uninterrupted sleep!

One reason the Abu Ghraib scandal has been so harmful is that the United States was revealed to be using, and even justifying, interrogation methods that the U.S. government continues to call torture when they are employed in other countries. The United States has been a powerful voice for victims of torture and human rights abuses around the world. When it violates the principles it preaches to others, its moral authority diminishes, and repressive governments find it much easier to resist American calls for change. Sure, State Department officials can continue to urge Saudi Arabia and Egypt and Algeria to treat people humanely, but when the governments of these countries can quote U.S. government memoranda to defend their brutal actions, what can an American diplomat say in response?

What makes all this even worse is that the Bush Administration has recognized—to its credit—that the promotion of human rights in the Middle East is critical to an effective, long-term campaign against terror. Repression in that region breeds radicalism and resentment. And when people are denied peaceful, democratic avenues to express their anger, they turn to the more violent alternatives terrorists offer. America's ability to champion human rights effectively has therefore never been more important to its security. But because of the prisoner abuse scandal, it has never been at greater risk. America's practices must be in line with its principles if America's policy of promoting democratic change around the world is to have a chance of succeeding.

TORTURE TECHNIQUES APPROVED BY THE UNITED STATES WHILE CONDEMNED IN OTHER COUNTRIES

Type of Abuse	Criticized by the United States as "Torture" in These Countries*	Approved by the United States
Binding/ Shackling of Limbs	China, Eritrea, Iraq, Israel, Libya, Pakistan	December 2, 2002: Secretary of Defense Donald Rumsfeld approved the use of "stress positions"; among techniques used was "short-shackling," in which the detainee is bound in painful positions for extended periods of time**
Stripping/ Forced Nudity	Egypt, North Korea, Syria, Turkey	December 2, 2002: Rumsfeld approved the removal of clothing**; according to Department of Defense internal investigations, forced nudity was widely employed in detention facilities in Afghanistan and Iraq
Solitary Confinement/ Isolation	China, Iran, Iraq, Jordan, North Korea, Pakistan, Tunisia, Turkey	December 2, 2002: Rumsfeld approved isolation of detainees for up to thirty days**; April 16, 2003: Rumsfeld affirmed approval of isolation with "detailed implementation instructions"; September 14, 2003: Lieutenant General Ricardo Sanchez, commander of U.S. forces in Iraq, approved isolation for up to thirty days—this period could be extended with permission of the Military Intelligence Brigade Commander; October 14, 2003: Combined Joint Task Force Seven, the U.S. military command in Baghdad (CJTF-7), approved isolation outside of a Coalition Provisional Authority holding facility, with permission of the Officer in Charge (OIC), with no maximum length of time given

Type of Abuse	Criticized by the United States as "Torture" in These Countries*	Approved by the United States
Threats of Dog Attacks	Libya	December 2, 2002: Rumsfeld approved the use of dogs to intimidate detainees in order to take advantage of individual phobias**; September 14, 2003: General Sanchez approved presence of military working dogs to exploit Arab fear of dogs; October 9, 2003: CJTF-7 approved presence of "working dogs" with permission of the OIC
Exposure to Excessive Heat/Cold	Eritrea, Indonesia, North Korea, Turkey	April 16, 2003:Rumsfeld approved "environmental manipulation," including adjusting temperature, and noted "consideration" should be given to the fact that courts in other countries have found this technique to be inhumane; September 14, 2003: General Sanchez approved environmental manipulation as well, noting same consideration as Rumsfeld; October 9, 2003: CJTF-7 approved environmental manipulation (gave example of low AC in summer, low heat in winter) with permission of OIC
Stress Positions: Forced Painful Positions or Repetitive Exercises	Burma, Iran, Israel, North Korea, Syria, Turkey	December 2, 2002: Rumsfeld approved stress positions for use for up to four hours, including "forced standing"**; September 14, 2003: General Sanchez approved use of stress positions for up to one hour per technique but could be continued for up to four hours with adequate rest; October 9, 2003: CJTF-7 approved use of stress positions for up to forty-five minutes within a four-hour time period with permission of the OIC
Sleep Deprivation	Indonesia, Iran, Israel, Jordan, Libya, Pakistan, Saudi Arabia, Tunisia, Turkey	December 2, 2002: Rumsfeld approved periods of interrogation that could last for up to twenty hours at a time**; September 14, 2003: General Sanchez approved "sleep management" that provided for a minimum of four hours of sleep in a twenty-four-hour time period, which could extend to seventy-

Type of Abuse	Criticized by the United States as "Torture" in These Countries*	Approved by the United States
		two hours total; October 9, 2003: CJTF-7 approved sleep management for up to seventy-two hours with permission of the OIC
Waterboarding: Submersion in Water or Dousing to Simulate Drowning	Brazil, Egypt, Syria, Tunisia	Alleged to have been approved for use by the Central Intelligence Agency***
Deprivation of Light: Blindfolding, Hooding, or Holding in Completely Darkened Surroundings	Egypt, Iran, Israel, Turkey	December 2, 2002: Rumsfeld approved "deprivation of light and auditory stimuli" as well as the use of hoods during transportation and interrogation**
Denial of Food/Water	Burma, Iraq, Libya, North Korea, Pakistan, Tunisia, Turkey, Zimbabwe	April 16, 2003: Rumsfeld approved "dietary manipulation" although "no intended deprivation of food or water"; September 14, 2003: General Sanchez approved dietary manipulation with the same caveat; October 9, 2003: CJTF-7 approved dietary manipulation, in which the detainee would be provided only a minimal amount of bread and water, with permission of the OIC

* The U.S. State Department publishes annual reports titled "Country Reports on Human Rights Practices" in which these countries, in successive recent reports, are described as perpetrating torture in these forms.

** In December 2002, this technique was approved by Secretary Rumsfeld, then rescinded by him on January 15, 2003, unless he granted permission in a specific case.

*** The New York Times reported on May 13, 2004, that "a technique known as 'water boarding,' in which a prisoner is strapped down, forcibly pushed under water and made to believe he might drown" was approved for use by the CIA.

12

THE ROAD TO ABU GHRAIB: TORTURE AND IMPUNITY IN U.S. DETENTION

Reed Brody

Reed Brody is Special Counsel at Human Rights Watch, where he led Human Rights Watch's intervention in the case against Augusto Pinochet and coordinates the prosecution of the former dictator of Chad, Hissène Habré, who was arrested on torture charges in Senegal. He is also the author of several reports on the abuse of prisoners in U.S. custody. This piece sets out the chain of events leading to torture of detainees in Afghanistan and Iraq, and the continuing lack of accountability for these crimes.

On April 28, 2004, Americans were shocked to see the first pictures of U.S. soldiers humiliating and torturing detainees at Abu Ghraib prison in Iraq. The pictures have since taken on iconic status: an Iraqi detainee draped in a hood and poncho, standing on a box, his arms outstretched, with wires attached to his extremities and genitals; a bored-looking female American soldier holding a naked Iraqi detainee lying at the end of a leash; naked and even dead Iraqi detainees in a variety of positions with American soldiers laughing and flashing thumbs up.

When the pictures first appeared, the United States government sought to portray the abuse as an isolated incident, the work of a few "bad apples" acting without orders. On May 4, U.S. Secretary of Defense Donald H. Rumsfeld, in a formulation that would be used over and over again by U.S. officials, described the abuses at Abu Ghraib as "an exceptional, isolated" case. In a nationally televised address on May

24, President George W. Bush spoke of "disgraceful conduct by a few American troops who dishonored our country and disregarded our values."

While some of the acts portrayed in the pictures can be attributed to individual or group sadism, the only truly exceptional aspect of the horrors at Abu Ghraib was that they were photographed. Detainees in U.S. custody in Afghanistan had experienced beatings, prolonged sleep and sensory deprivation, forced nakedness, and humiliation as early as 2001. Comparable—and, indeed, more extreme—cases of torture and inhuman treatment had been extensively documented by the International Committee of the Red Cross and by journalists at numerous locations in Iraq outside Abu Ghraib.

As became increasingly obvious in the months after the "scandal" came to public light, this pattern of abuse did not result from the acts of individual soldiers who broke the rules. It resulted from decisions made by the Bush Administration to bend, ignore, or cast rules aside. Administration policies created the climate for Abu Ghraib in three fundamental ways.

First, in the aftermath of the September 11 attacks on the United States, the Bush Administration seemingly determined that winning the war on terror required that the United States circumvent international law. "There was a before–9/11 and an after–9/11," said Cofer Black, former director of the CIA's counterterrorist unit, in testimony to Congress. "After 9/11 the gloves came off." [1] Senior administration lawyers in a series of internal memos argued over the objections of career military and State Department counsel that the new war against terrorism rendered "obsolete" long-standing legal restrictions on the treatment and interrogation of detainees.

The administration effectively sought to rewrite the Geneva Conventions of 1949 to eviscerate many of their most important protections. These included the rights of all detainees in an armed conflict to

be free from humiliating and degrading treatment, as well as from torture and other forms of coercive interrogation. The Pentagon and the
Justice Department developed the breathtaking legal argument that the
president, as commander-in-chief of the armed forces, was not bound
by U.S. or international laws prohibiting torture when acting to protect
national security, and that such laws might even be unconstitutional if
they hampered the war on terror. The United States began to create offshore, off-limits, prisons such as Guantánamo Bay, Cuba, maintained
other detainees in "undisclosed locations," and without any legal due
process sent terrorism suspects to countries where information was
beaten out of them.

White House legal counsel (and now attorney general) Alberto
Gonzales, while suggesting that the Geneva Conventions be circum-
vented, did convey to President Bush the worries of military leaders that
these policies might "undermine U.S. military culture, which empha-
sizes maintaining the highest standards of conduct in combat and could
introduce an element of uncertainty in the status of adversaries." Those
warnings were ignored, but proved justified. In May 2004, a member of
the 377th Military Police Company told the *New York Times* that the
labeling of prisoners in Afghanistan as "enemy combatants" not subject
to the Geneva Conventions contributed to their abuse. "We were pretty
much told that they were nobodies, that they were just enemy combatants," he said. "I think that giving them the distinction of soldier would
have changed our attitudes toward them." [2]

Second, the United States began to employ coercive methods designed to "soften up" detainees for interrogation. Secretary Rumsfeld
approved a series of such techniques for use at Guantánamo, including
the use of guard dogs to induce fear in prisoners, hooding them, and re-
moving their clothes—which violate not only the Geneva Conventions
but the laws against torture and other prohibited ill-treatment.

As early as October 2001, after the capture in Afghanistan of John

Walker Lindh, the so-called "American Taliban," a Navy admiral reportedly told the officer interrogating Lindh that "the secretary of Defense's counsel has authorized him to 'take the gloves off' and ask whatever he wanted."[3] Lindh was stripped naked in the Afghan cold, taped to a stretcher, and questioned for days on end. According to documents shown to the *Los Angeles Times,* Lindh's responses were cabled back to the Defense Department as often as hourly.

The U.S. Central Intelligence Agency was also given the authority to "disappear" certain prisoners, placing leading Al Qaeda suspects in long-term secret incommunicado detention in "undisclosed locations." The CIA's "disappeared" prisoners, who have gone years without access to their families, lawyers, governments, or the International Committee of the Red Cross (ICRC), include Khalid Shaikh Mohammed, the principal architect of the September 11 attacks; Abu Zubaydah, a close aide of Osama bin Laden's; Ramzi bin al-Shibh, who but for his failure to get a U.S. visa might have been one of the 9/11 hijackers; and Abd al-Rahim al-Nashiri, the alleged mastermind of the USS *Cole* bombing.[4] There are persistent reports that these "disappeared" detainees have been physically tortured. The *New York Times* and the *Washington Post* have reported that Khalid Shaikh Mohammed has been subjected to the "waterboarding" technique—known in Latin America as the *"submarino"*—in which the detainee is strapped down, forcibly pushed under water, and made to believe he might drown. Mohammed's seven- and nine-year-old sons were also picked up, presumably to induce him to talk.

These techniques, familiar to victims of torture in many of the world's most repressive dictatorships, are forbidden by prohibitions against torture and other cruel, inhuman, or degrading treatment not only by the Geneva Conventions but by other international instruments to which the United States is a party and by the U.S. military's own long-standing regulations.

The CIA also stepped up a program of "extraordinary renditions," sending detainees to countries in the Middle East, including Egypt and Syria, known to practice torture routinely.

Two Pentagon panels would find that the practices approved by Secretary Rumsfeld for use at Guantánamo, though later withdrawn, had "migrated" to Afghanistan and Iraq, where they were used systematically. Obviously, the purpose of these techniques is to inflict pain, suffering, and severe humiliation on detainees. Once that purpose was legitimized by military and intelligence officials, it is not surprising that ordinary soldiers came to believe that even more extreme forms of abuse were acceptable. The brazenness with which some soldiers conducted themselves at Abu Ghraib, snapping photographs and flashing the "thumbs-up" sign as they abused prisoners, confirms that they felt they had nothing to hide from their superiors.

Third, until the publication of the Abu Ghraib photographs forced action, Bush Administration officials took at best a "see no evil, hear no evil" approach to reports of detainee mistreatment. From the earliest days of the war in Afghanistan and the occupation of Iraq, the U.S. government has been aware of allegations of abuse. Yet high-level pledges of humane treatment were never implemented with specific orders or guidelines to forbid coercive methods of interrogation. Investigations of deaths in custody languished; soldiers and intelligence personnel accused of abuse, including all cases involving the killing of detainees, escaped judicial punishment. When, in the midst of the worst abuses, the ICRC complained to Coalition forces, Army officials apparently responded by trying to curtail the ICRC's access. Concern for the basic rights of persons taken into custody in Afghanistan and Iraq did not factor into the Bush Administration's agenda. The administration largely dismissed expressions of concern for their treatment, from both within the government and outside. This, too, sent a message to those dealing with detainees in the field about the priorities of those in command.

The severest abuses at Abu Ghraib occurred in the immediate after-math of a decision by Secretary Rumsfeld to step up the hunt for "ac-tionable intelligence" among Iraqi prisoners. The officer who oversaw intelligence gathering at Guantánamo, Major General Geoffrey Miller, was brought in to overhaul interrogation practices in Iraq, and teams of interrogators from Guantánamo were sent to Abu Ghraib. Following General Miller's visit, the commanding general in Iraq, Lieutenant Gen-eral Ricardo S. Sanchez, issued orders to "manipulate an internee's emotions and weaknesses" and specifically approved illegal interroga-tion methods—including the use of unmuzzled guard dogs to frighten prisoners—which were then applied by soldiers at Abu Ghraib. Military police were ordered by military intelligence to "set physical and mental conditions for favorable interrogation of witnesses." The captain who oversaw interrogations at the Afghan detention center where two pris-oners died in detention posted "Interrogation Rules of Engagement" at Abu Ghraib, authorizing coercive methods (with prior written approval of the military commander)—including the use of military guard dogs to instill fear—that violate the Geneva Conventions and the Conven-tion against Torture and Other Cruel, Inhuman or Degrading Treat-ment or Punishment.

Unlike U.S. actions in the global campaign against terrorism, the armed conflict in Iraq was justified in part on the basis of bringing democracy and respect for the rule of law to an Iraqi population long suffering under Saddam Hussein. Abusive treatment used against terror-ism suspects after September 11 came to be considered permissible by the United States in an armed conflict to suppress resistance to a mili-tary occupation.

The Bush Administration apparently believed that the new wars it was fighting could not be won if it was constrained by "old" rules. The disturbing information that has come to light points to an official policy of torture and cruel, inhuman, or degrading treatment.

Ironically, the administration is losing the war for hearts and minds around the world precisely because it threw those rules out. Rather than advance the war on terror, the widespread prisoner abuse has damaged efforts to build global support for countering terrorism. As the September 11 Commission said, "Allegations that the United States abused prisoners in its custody make it harder to build the diplomatic, political, and military alliances the government will need."[5] Indeed, the iconic pictures from Abu Ghraib are—like the pictures of orange-suited detainees at Guantánamo—being used as recruiting posters for jihad. Policies adopted to make the United States more secure from terrorism have in fact made it more vulnerable.

The Road From Abu Ghraib

Shortly after the Abu Ghraib photos came out, President Bush vowed that the "wrongdoers will be brought to justice."

In fact, however, the only wrongdoers being brought to justice for crimes against detainees in U.S. custody around the world are those at the bottom of the chain of command. Indeed, the United States continues to do what dictatorships and banana republics do the world over (and what the United States has traditionally decried when they do)—shift blame downward.

As of this writing only one officer higher than the rank of sergeant—a major—has been charged with a crime. No civilian leader at the Pentagon or the CIA has been investigated.

The Pentagon established no fewer than seven investigations in the wake of Abu Ghraib.[6] Yet none had the independence or the breadth to get to the bottom of the scandal. Almost all of them involved the military investigating itself, and each was focused on only one aspect or another of the treatment of detainees. None of the military probes was aimed higher up the chain of command than General Sanchez. None of the investigations had the task of examining the role of the CIA or of civilian authorities.

The first report, released by Army Inspector General Lieutenant General Paul Mikolashek was nothing less than a whitewash. After reviewing ninety-four confirmed cases of detainee abuse in Afghanistan and Iraq, Mikolashek concluded—in keeping with the government line—that the abuses did not result from any policy and were not the fault of senior officers but rather were "unauthorized actions taken by a few individuals." Imagine if China or Russia released a similar report.

Two subsequent reports, one by a panel named by Rumsfeld and headed by former defense secretary James Schlesinger, the other a probe of the 205th Military Intelligence Brigade at Abu Ghraib by Generals Anthony R. Jones and George Fay contained important and disturbing information on the torture and mistreatment of prisoners in Afghanistan, Iraq, and Guantánamo. The Fay/Jones report detailed forty-four cases of prisoner abuse at Abu Ghraib alone.

The reports also provided evidence that policies approved in Washington and at the command level led to abuses on the ground. The Schlesinger report noted that "the augmented techniques [approved by Secretary Rumsfeld] for Guantánamo migrated to Afghanistan and Iraq where they were neither limited nor safeguarded." It found that "pressure for additional intelligence and the more aggressive methods sanctioned by the Secretary of Defense memorandum resulted in stronger interrogation techniques. They did contribute to a belief that stronger interrogation methods were needed and appropriate in their treatment of detainees." General Jones found that "policy memoranda promulgated by the CJTF-7 Commander [General Sanchez] led indirectly to some of the non-violent and non-sexual abuses" at Abu Ghraib.

Yet both reports shied away from the logical conclusion that high-level military and civilian officials should be fully investigated for their role in the crimes committed at Abu Ghraib and elsewhere. The

Schlesinger report talked about "management" failures when it should have been more forthright about policy failures. Indeed, it seemed to go out of its way to not find any relationship between Secretary Rumsfeld's approval of interrogation techniques designed to inflict pain and humiliation and the widespread mistreatment and torture of detainees in Iraq, Afghanistan, and Guantánamo. The use of guard dogs is one example. Mr. Rumsfeld's authorization of dogs to frighten prisoners was unprecedented. Yet, as the Schlesinger panel revealed, "exploiting fear of dogs" became an interrogation tactic in Afghanistan as well. The panel also confirmed that, in September 2003, just before the three months of what Secretary Schlesinger described as "sadism on the night shift" at Abu Ghraib, and at a time when Washington was pressing interrogators to "produce 'actionable intelligence,' " General Sanchez issued orders, "using reasoning" from President Bush's February 2002 memo, in which he unilaterally declared some prisoners "unlawful combatants," and told interrogators to "exploit Arab fear of dogs while maintaining security during interrogations." Although this order was later sent back by the U.S. Central Command, and rewritten to require General Sanchez to preapprove the use of dogs, guard dogs featured prominently in abuses at Abu Ghraib.

General Fay was adamant that "when dogs are used to threaten and terrify detainees, there is a clear violation of applicable laws and regulations." Yet this was exactly what Secretary Rumsfeld formally approved as an interrogation tactic in Guantánamo, what General Sanchez approved for Abu Ghraib, and what soldiers did in both Afghanistan and Iraq.[7] Neither Secretary Rumsfeld nor General Sanchez are the subjects of criminal investigations. Similarly, despite mounting reports of the CIA's "disappearance" and alleged torture of detainees and the growing evidence regarding the torture of detainees rendered by the CIA, there appears to be no move to investigate former CIA director George Tenet.

It is entirely appropriate that those soldiers directly involved in using guard dogs on detainees and in other forms of abuse in Iraq and Afghanistan be prosecuted. No orders they may have received can relieve them of their responsibility for manifestly illegal actions. But the privates and sergeants are not the ones who cast aside the Geneva Conventions, or who authorized the use of illegal interrogation methods. True accountability requires that those at higher levels who approved or tolerated crimes against detainees also be brought to justice.

If there is no real accountability at the command level for the widespread abuses against detainees in Iraq and Afghanistan, the perpetrators of atrocities around the world will point to the United States' behavior to blunt any criticism of their own abuses. All the protestations of disgust and condemnation by President Bush and others will be meaningless. The stain of Abu Ghraib will remain on the U.S. flag.

13

RESPECTING THE GENEVA CONVENTIONS

John McCain

U.S. Senator John McCain began his career as a naval aviator and received honors including the Silver Star, the Bronze Star, the Legion of Merit, the Purple Heart, and the Distinguished Flying Cross. In 1967, he was shot down over Vietnam and held as a prisoner of war in Hanoi for five and a half years, much of it in solitary confinement. Some of his fellow prisoners were tortured and even killed. This article, originally published in the Wall Street Journal, *sets out why the Geneva Conventions remain a vital protection against torture, and also why the United States must hold itself to a higher standard of wartime conduct than terrorists do.*

Since the abuses at Abu Ghraib have come to light, American leaders at all levels have rightly expressed outrage and contrition. Yet there also exists an undercurrent of sentiment that seeks to fault America's strict adherence to international humanitarian law, and to blame the organizations that monitor its implementation.

In recent days, some have labeled Red Cross personnel as "humanitarian do-gooders" whose presence in coalition-run detention centers is inappropriate while American soldiers are fighting and dying. Others have warned that the ICRC is on the path toward becoming a left-wing advocacy group, and portrayed the Geneva Conventions as a hindrance to our ability to extract intelligence from prisoners that might save U.S. lives.

It is critical to realize that the Red Cross and the Geneva Conventions do not endanger American soldiers, they protect them. Our soldiers enter battle with the knowledge that should they be taken prisoner, there are laws intended to protect them and impartial international observers to inquire after them.

America's observance of the Geneva Conventions and our support for the ICRC in part determines the willingness of other nations to do the same. While our intelligence personnel in Abu Ghraib may have believed that they were protecting U.S. lives by roughing up detainees to extract information, they have had the opposite effect. Their actions have increased the danger to American soldiers, in this conflict and in future wars.

There are, of course, some enemies who will never be constrained by the Geneva Conventions, and who will never permit ICRC access to captured Americans. If Al Qaeda beheads kidnapped Americans, some argue, why must we be bound to treat detained members of Al Qaeda humanely?

When the principle of reciprocity does not apply, we must instead remember the principles by which our nation conducts its affairs. America is a nation of laws, and we hold ourselves to a higher standard than those of the terrorists. We distinguish ourselves from our enemies by our treatment of our enemies. Were we to abandon the principles of wartime conduct to which we have freely committed ourselves, we would lose the moral standing that has made America unique in the world.

Some also have argued that the Geneva Conventions have been rendered quaint by the new circumstances in which we find ourselves. We do face a new enemy in the global war on terror, and much of our ability to disrupt attacks and destroy terrorist cells depends on the quality of intelligence we gather from detainees. Yet nothing in the Conventions precludes directed interrogations. They do, however, prohibit torture and humiliation of detainees, whether or not they are deemed POWs.

These are standards that are never obsolete—they cut to the heart of how moral people must treat other human beings. They also are the principles on which the liberation of Iraq is based. We are bringing to Iraq a new day, an era that is better in all ways than the tyranny of Saddam Hussein. This era replaces terror, humiliation, and arbitrary rule with freedom, human rights, and the rule of law.

The Red Cross and other "do-gooders" help us achieve this goal. Attacks on the integrity of the ICRC damage the credibility of its pledge to respect its confidentiality agreements with governments. Without this credibility, parties engaged in conflict will be increasingly reluctant to provide the Red Cross with humanitarian access, including its visits to prisoners of war. When Americans are held captive by enemy forces, these visits can be critical to their physical and mental health.

Rather than placing blame on the ICRC or other humanitarian groups, we must instead fix our gaze on those individuals who perpetrated abuses at Abu Ghraib. Had American officials paid heed earlier to ICRC reports of these abuses at Abu Ghraib, we could have limited the damage these individuals have done to America's international standing. Only by prosecuting these individuals, in the letter and spirit of the Geneva Conventions, can we remove the stain on those 2.3 million men and women in the U.S. armed forces who consider such behavior entirely un-American.

14

COMMAND RESPONSIBILITY FOR TORTURE

Dinah Pokempner

As General Counsel for Human Rights Watch, Dinah Pokempner supervises policy on issues of international law, including establishing international legal tribunals, setting international standards, drafting legislation, and guiding legal reform initiatives in various countries. She has conducted research on human rights in Cambodia, Hong Kong, Vietnam, and former Yugoslavia. Her piece examines the psychological dynamic of torture, command responsibility, the norms against torture, and the subtle ways in which permission to torture is conveyed.

At this point, there are few people outside the Bush cabinet who think the abuses to which U.S. personnel subjected prisoners at Abu Ghraib and elsewhere were solely the responsibility of a few kids on the night shift. One after another formerly classified government memorandum has revealed a high-level anticipation and planning of practices that have always been known to be cruel, inhuman, and degrading, and even torturous.

Yet no sanction has ever followed for the higher echelons of leadership in the United States. President Bush was reelected; Secretary of Defense Donald Rumsfeld was reappointed after telling the Senate that he accepted full responsibility for the scandals; Jay Bybee, who sought to define "torture" so narrowly that pulling fingernails wouldn't qualify, sits comfortably on the federal bench; and Alberto Gonzales is the U.S. Attorney General, after endorsing violations of international law and advising how to escape liability.

What was the relationship between the classified memoranda and closed-door meetings, on the one hand, and on the other the pervasive abuses of prisoners in American hands? Reporters kept calling Human Rights Watch to see if we had some signed order for torture, "a smoking gun" to prove superior responsibility, even while there seemed to be nothing but thick smoke everywhere. The gap between our common-sense understanding of how the administration facilitated torture and its own denial of responsibility is provocative. What is torture's dynamic? How do guards get the signal from above that torture may be expected or at least tolerated? And how can we guarantee no future Abu Ghraibs if there are no consequences for leaders?

Any notion of political, moral, and legal responsibility turns on what we knew, or should have known, to be the likely results of our actions. And as it happens, we know a great deal about torture, what factors make it likely to transpire, and how hard it is to limit or regulate. We also know a great deal about the subtle ways in which permission to torture is conveyed. Physical and psychological abuse are a predictable risk in certain situations of group conformity, hierarchy, and stress, as anyone who has encountered a fraternity, a class of military recruits, a prison ward, or even a slumber party well knows, and there are very specific precautions that can mitigate the risk. Holding our political and military leaders to this standard of real-world knowledge will not tie their hands in waging war or combating terrorism. But it is essential to restore integrity to our values and laws.

The Normality of Torture

Torture has since ancient times been a means of criminal investigation. But its purposes go far beyond the extraction of confessions or investigative leads. "Classical" or premodern practices of torture were often public and explicitly symbolic: thieves had their hands chopped off, adulterers were stoned to death by the community, apostates and witches were burned at the stake, lashes and slashes were calibrated to the degree of the offense. Sometimes people were tortured "for their own good," to save their souls while destroying their bodies; torture was literally about refashioning the victim. Torture was also part of constructing the enemy—the individual was tortured to demonstrate how dangerous, subhuman, or weak he or she was, to render that person into an animal, or infantile, or broken state. Torture could serve the purpose of venting fear and anger or asserting control in war, when combatants must contend with mortal danger and the death of their own colleagues. Such functions were didactic, often public, aimed at conveying messages to the dominant group as well as intimidating the victim's community.

In the modern era, the rationale for torture has mainly changed from viewing it as an acceptable open and didactic practice to considering it a forbidden and covert exercise in intelligence-gathering. The "science" of torture and similar abusive treatment has developed to break the physical and mental resistance of subjects before they expire or go mad and thus become useless as sources of information. As the norm against torture grew stronger, especially in democracies, forms of torture that did not leave lasting visible marks became more popular and widespread; hence the prevalence of stress positions or sleep deprivation, techniques that when prolonged can cause the complete mental or physical breakdown, or even death, of the victim, but leave little or no physical evidence.[1]

But while torture has gone behind doors, its older purposes and functions have not disappeared. Torture is still about domination and communication—expressing the torturer's anger, contempt, and even fear; intimidating those in the victim's immediate circle, be that the cell-block or family or town; teaching new personnel who the enemy is and how to handle him; bonding a group through ritual humiliation of others; and even refashioning the victim to the torturer's conception, as in the case of imposing sexual humiliation on the supposedly sex-obsessed Arab male, or shaving the mujahedeen's alien beard, or "converting" the fundamentalist through hours of forced positioning to "cooperate" and be rewarded by an American military-base hamburger.

"Clinical" torture, the idea that there is a cold science to imposing just the precise amount of pain necessary to extract the needed information, is a myth. However much the torturer wishes to see him or herself as professional and disengaged, torture is an intimate act that engages the torturer's own emotions and imagination. This may be why it is so difficult to control. Yet official torturers are not usually sadists or psychologically aberrational, as such persons would be susceptible to letting their proclivities get in the way of extracting reliable intelligence. Torture, rather, is a "normal" act by "normal" people in certain circumstances and conditions.

Researchers in psychology and social science have documented these circumstances and conditions extensively, starting with Stanley Milgram's experiments that demonstrated the willingness of normal people to inflict what seemed to be excruciatingly painful electric shocks on what they took to be research subjects in learning experiments. Philip Zimbardo elaborated this research, showing how psychologically ordinary students at Berkeley could transform themselves into sadistic "prison guards" in a matter of days, given simply the task of keeping order among other students denominated as "prisoners."

These and many other studies[2] have examined exactly what circumstances facilitate or inhibit abusive behavior. The basic recipe includes elements such as a hierarchical situation, where those with power to inflict abuse have socially acceptable roles (teacher, guard, interrogator), an acceptable rationale for harsh behavior (instruction, controlling dangerous people, obtaining life-saving information), a commitment to employ the harsh behavior where called for and basic rules to do so, and diffusion of responsibility if harm results (following orders, the complicity of many in the project). Yet other ingredients that increase the likelihood of abuse include the deindividuation of those with power (wearing uniforms, not revealing names), the dehumanization of those subject to abuse (using epithets or in other ways making them seem subhuman), the perceived compliance of others to the "duty" of using harsh actions, and the socialization to abusive treatment by introducing it in incremental steps.

Wartime detention of the enemy is an obvious petri dish for abuse, and the wars in Iraq and Afghanistan, cast as sorties against global "terrorism," richly provided these sorts of facilitating elements. The enemy was constantly reviled by the highest leaders as "terrorist" or "evil," fighting lawlessly and therefore outside the protection of the law. As the battles in Iraq and Afghanistan proved tough, enormous pressure was applied from the top down to obtain intelligence, a purpose whose end (saving the lives of U.S. forces and civilians) served to rationalize repugnant means. We now know that hundreds participated in or witnessed the abuses, that officers and medical personnel must have been complicit, and that what few whistle-blowers emerged were threatened or ignored.

Signaling Tolerance

Because torture is taboo, entailing criminal liability the world over, orders to torture are rarely explicit. Superiors more typically indicate the desired result—to obtain intelligence, to "break" the prisoner—and subordinates understand what means would be expected or tolerated to that end. In a culture such as the U.S. military, where the prohibition on abuse of prisoners has been explicit for some time, we need to look at countervailing signals from the top over a period of time to understand how subordinates came to read the official attitude as permissive. Putting aside the classified discussions of the legality of torture and the often-revised internal lists of permitted interrogation techniques, even the administration's public statements sent several messages that overwhelmed the norm of humane treatment. These were: this war can't be fought under the old rules; the enemy is dangerous/subhuman; and there may be times when brutality is warranted.

The context of statements is important to decoding their meaning or probable interpretation. In the days following 9/11, senior administration officials relentlessly sounded the theme that terrorism demanded a response outside the traditional paradigm of war. Vice President Dick Cheney said on NBC's *Meet the Press,* "We also have to work, though, sort of the dark side, if you will. . . . A lot of what needs to be done here will have to be done quietly . . . using sources and methods that are available to our intelligence agencies. . . . It is a mean, nasty, dangerous, dirty business out there, and we have to operate in that arena." [3] Bush on September 19 echoed these words, saying, "The mind-set of war must change. It is a different type of battle." [4] The idea that the Geneva Conventions were "quaint" or "obsolete" in the war against terror, expressed in Alberto Gonzales's now-famous classified memorandum, can be read as a legal reflection of attitudes that the highest leaders were voicing much earlier.

In this context, statements of leaders at key moments of decision took on a great deal of meaning as to how the enemy was to be treated when captured. One key moment was the decision to term prisoners in Afghanistan "enemy combatants" rather than "POWs," with the (as it happens, false) implication that they were not covered by the Geneva Conventions and that only presidential discretion, and not law, entitled them to "humane treatment." A member of the 377th Military Police Company told the *New York Times* in May 2004, "We were pretty much told that they were nobodies, that they were just enemy combatants. I think that giving them the distinction of soldier would have changed our attitudes toward them." [5]

Moreover, to the extent that there were high-level affirmations that detainees were to be treated humanely, these were usually qualified or conditioned in such a way as to muddy the message or undermine it entirely. When the first photographs of detainees arriving at Guantánamo appeared, showing them shackled, kneeling, in some cases in goggles, hoods, or mittens, Rumsfeld denied that there had been any mistreatment in transit. "Technically unlawful combatants *do not have any rights under the Geneva Convention.* We have indicated that we do plan to, *for the most part,* treat them in a manner that is *reasonably* consistent with the Geneva Conventions, *to the extent that they're appropriate. . . ."* (emphasis added). At the same press conference, General Richard Myers reminded reporters that "these are very dangerous people. These are people that would gnaw through hydraulic lines to bring [a plane] down. These are very dangerous people and that's how they're being treated. . . . We're going to try to do our best to treat them humanely, at the same time realizing they're very dangerous people."[6] Anyone suffering from cognitive dissonance as to whether the detainees were to be treated as human beings or as savage beasts no doubt got the cue as to the direction in which to resolve the contradiction.

Yet another key moment was when Major General Geoffrey Miller, in charge of stepping up interrogation techniques in Guantánamo, visited Abu Ghraib to do the same. Brigadier General Janis Karpinski recalled that Miller told her that detainees "are like dogs, and if you allow them to believe at any point that they are more than a dog then you've lost control of them."[7] There are odd reverberations of this message in the exploitation of fear of dogs as an explicitly approved technique until April 2003, and in the Abu Ghraib photographs of a female guard holding a male prisoner on a leash and prisoners being menaced by dogs. The signal of approval apparently traveled more swiftly and more deeply than the signal of disapproval.

Metaphor is powerful at evoking emotion and conveying a world of meaning, a quality recognized by cognitive linguists and politicians

alike. Wild West imagery often dominated Bush's discourse, from repeated vows that terrorists "can run but can't hide," to a vigilante-style
call for Osama bin Laden "dead or alive." [8] The president often resorted
to the epithet "terrorist" (and sometimes "barbarian" or "evildoer") to
describe the enemy, regardless of whether it was Al Qaeda, the Taliban,
or the Iraqi resistance. It is not implausible that the reason novel interrogation techniques migrated to Iraq along with specific troops and commanders is the lack of consistent distinction that was prevalent in public
statements at the highest levels.

Perhaps no metaphor so vividly expresses the hardened attitude toward intelligence-gathering as Cofer Black's testimony before Congress
that "After 9/11 the gloves came off." [9] Indeed, according to a *Los Angeles Times* story of June 9, 2004, after an Army intelligence officer began
to question John Walker Lindh, a Navy admiral told the intelligence officer that "the secretary of Defense's counsel has authorized him to 'take
the gloves off' and ask whatever he wanted." According to Lindh's lawyer, at this time his client was being questioned while propped up
naked, bound to a stretcher, held in freezing conditions, and being denied pain medication. Mark Danner reported a military intelligence
captain showed him e-mails he sent to colleagues in August 2003 where
he tried to define "unlawful combatants" and promised to provide
guidance on their interrogation, soliciting his correspondents for their
"wish list" of interrogation techniques for this category of detainee. The
captain reportedly closed his messages by saying, "The gloves are coming off, gentlemen, regarding these detainees, Col Boltz has made it
clear that we want these individuals broken." [10] A subsequent *Washington
Post* report noted that this message for "wish lists" was widely circulated
in the Iraq theater. The query and its vivid language seem to have pen-
etrated deeply, signaling new latitude, for incidents of serious abuse
transpired shortly thereafter. A military intelligence staff sergeant, repri-
manded for supervising the severe beating of one detainee, replied,

"This situation is made worse with messages from higher echelons soliciting lists of alternative interrogation techniques and the usage of phrases such as 'the gloves are coming off.' "[11]

You do not have to be a cognitive linguist to know that this phrase, coming out of the mouths of military officers—rather than, say, debutantes—conveys a meaning more along the lines of "use brass knuckles" or "beat them bloody if you have to" than "let's not stand on ceremony" or "don't be shy." Coming from the world of boxing, the phrase clearly conveys the sense of fighting outside the rules, without regard to the harm inflicted—about as apt a summary of official policy toward "enemy combatants" as one could express in vernacular terms.

Of course, impunity is one of the strongest signals of all. Mistreatment of detainees in Afghanistan, Guantánamo, and Iraq was widespread, and entailed hundreds of perpetrators, witnesses, and collaborators. The International Committee of the Red Cross raised these issues strongly, and human rights groups demanded investigation, with little result. The fact is, almost no incidents received serious public investigation until the Abu Ghraib photographs became known.

The Norm Against Torture

Torture is globally ubiquitous, and yet the norm against torture is arguably the most absolute in all international human rights law. The state may not torture in times of war or other national emergency, for any purpose whatsoever, no matter how many other lives may be at stake.[12] Numerous treaties reflect this obligation, which has become so fundamental and universal that it is deemed to bind all states, regardless of consent, as a peremptory norm. That torture occurs regularly is not an argument for exceptions to the norm, any more than the ubiquity of rape is an argument to craft limited circumstances where rape may be authorized or immunized. Understanding the nature of torture, however, illuminates why its prohibition is absolute.

Unlike a surgical procedure or a research methodology, torture is not easily susceptible to precision and restraint in application. Its internal dynamic makes it prone to ever wider use. Victims become inured to pain, inviting ever harsher and more imaginative measures, and no interrogator wants to "soften up" a subject just to have the next guy on the shift get the payoff when the prisoner cracks. The very commission of brutality engages the emotions, impelling the torturer to resolve ambivalence toward seeing the victim as ever more deserving of harsh treatment, as we see in the taunts of female guards toward prisoners who urinated on themselves from fear of guard dogs. Torture, like power, appears to be habit-forming. The rationale of torture in an age of terror—averting imminent and massive harm to civilians by torturing the right source—easily slides to cover ever more remote sources and more hypothetical harms. It is difficult to torture just a little.

In short, there is much about torture that militates against "pinpoint" application; once tolerated for some limited purpose, torture tends to spread like ink on wet paper. The example of Israel is instructive, and not only because the limited authorization of physically coercive interrogation rapidly devolved into widespread torture prior to the 1999 Israeli Supreme Court ban. After that decision, which outlawed coercive interrogation but left open one tiny loophole—a "necessity" defense for officials being prosecuted for torture—the government had acknowledged by mid-2002 using "physical pressure" in ninety cases, and independent research suggested there were hundreds more, with no official investigation ever resulting in a decision to prosecute.[13]

With this understanding, the norm against torture cannot be read as merely "negative," requiring the state to refrain from certain acts. Rather, it is an injunction to a great many positive acts, especially in situations such as war. Just as we know the many facilitating conditions, the elements that inhibit torture and related abuse are also known.

The International Committee of the Red Cross conducted a study of the key factors that impel combatants to commit violations of international humanitarian law and the implications for preventative measures. It identified many of the elements noted above, drawing from the works of these social psychologists as well as large-scale surveys of civilians and combatants. With regard to preventative measures, it concluded that knowledge of the law was not enough to inhibit abuse. War invariably entails military hierarchy, group conformity, and some degree of moral disengagement toward the enemy (whom soldiers are ordered to kill). In this situation, trying to change individual attitudes is less effective and relevant than ensuring that training, strict orders, and sanctions all support lawful behavior.[14] Human Rights Watch has documented that the actual monitoring and sanctioning of misbehavior by trusted superior officers is the most effective deterrent in situations of hazing or prison abuse.[15] While the law would not excuse any individual from responsibility for torture because his or her superiors failed to take enough precautions, such a failure may widen the circle of those responsible.

Thinking about Responsibility

The most striking feature of the scandal so far has been the relative lack of consequence to those in high position. While there are various theories of responsibility—moral, political, and legal—the very concept of responsibility entails the potential for consequence, be it public opprobrium, reprimand, discipline, dismissal, disqualification, economic sanction, or loss of freedom. Indeed, there is a sense that just as the Office of Legal Counsel sought to calculate the risk of legal liability for torture, so other political offices have calculated the social and political fallout from the scandal and concluded no further action need be taken. It may be that the official effort to divorce responsibility from any consequence may be the most damaging product of the whole experience, for it amounts to a conscious construction of impunity.[16]

A key question in thinking about responsibility from any point of view is the question of what leaders can be said to know about the probable results of their acts or inaction. Acts whose consequences are truly unforeseeable do not entail intention or volition of the harmful result, and for that reason we rarely impose severe consequences. Bureaucracy is a complicating factor in this sort of analysis, as one person's actions may not alone give rise to harm, but those acts may be subject to yet further actions by others that do.[17] As Donald Rumsfeld said to Larry King:

> You know, the—what was going on in the midnight shift in Abu Ghraib Prison halfway across the world is something that clearly someone in Washington, D.C., can't manage or deal with. And so I have no regrets.

But in situations of organizational hierarchy, the risk of abusive follow-on actions can be quite foreseeable, and preventable. This is what lies behind the legal doctrine of command or superior responsibility.

This doctrine holds leaders liable for the unlawful actions of their subordinates where they had the authority to exercise command and control, where the leaders knew or should have known that the subordinates were committing, had committed, or were about to commit the acts, and where the leaders failed to take steps to prevent or punish such abuses. It is worth noting from the outset that this is a narrow standard, drawn for the imposition of criminal penalties, and there may be many cases of blameworthy action that fall outside. For example, we may still want to hold officials politically responsible for acts that bore a foreseeable and causal relation to abuse by others, even where those others were not in the direct chain of command and control. The question of command authority is often critical, especially for officials who are not at the apex of a bureaucracy. When we look at the highest leaders, often quite distant from the actual perpetrators of abuse, our attention tends to focus on what they knew or should have known, and what they did or did not do with that knowledge.

The evidence so far is that acts of abuse by American forces in the field were rampant from the first months of the Afghanistan invasion and by 2003 reported in the press and by NGOs; that the treatment of detainees sent to Guantánamo was abusive enough to warrant protest by the International Committee of the Red Cross and even the Federal Bureau of Investigation; and that physical abuse, sexual abuse, humiliation, and even murder took place at the hands of U.S. forces all over Iraq, not just in Abu Ghraib. Independent investigation might reveal how widely these facts and complaints were known at higher levels of the administration and armed forces. At the same time, those higher levels were making decisions about specific coercive techniques, as well as the parameters of international obligations on torture and cruel, inhuman, and degrading treatment.

The administration would have us take these developments in the field and the developments in Washington as unrelated. And indeed, its conception of the entire Iraq venture seems to have been characterized by much wishful thinking and repression of factual impediments. But if we assume that leaders should know something about what facilitates or inhibits torture and ill-treatment, a complete disjunction seems less likely. At the very least, we would expect that leaders would be aware that permission to engage in some hitherto forbidden practices might invite experimentation with yet others, that the subtle distinctions between the detention regime for POWs and "enemy combatants" might be lost on forces that at the same time were pressured to produce intelligence, that the political rhetoric demonizing the enemy could impel demonic behavior if unchecked by a demonstrated will to prevent and punish mistreatment. Indeed, if we ascribe to the rest of the leadership this sort of commonsense knowledge, their actions appear less naïve and more "a conscious decision to create an atmosphere of ambiguity in which experimentation with . . . unlawful interrogation techniques . . . could occur." [18] And as one after another internal investigation fails to hold superiors accountable, even as ever more facts of abuse come to light, the responsibility of those at the highest level for inaction and fostering impunity only accrues.

Epilogue

The backlash to this real-world narrative of responsibility is well under way.[19] Its most cogent thrust is that the absolute nature of the norm is somehow at fault. Apologists for physical coercion on the left and the right argue that unless the United States can apply potent means in interrogation, including exploiting uncertainty of how far it might really go in torture, it will not be able to prevent attacks that could harm innocent civilians, including mass attacks.

But that argument requires us to believe we live in an entirely different world than has ever existed at any time or place. The idea that torture produces safety is much contested. Torture and cruelty beget enemies and alienate allies, and while maltreatment may produce usable information in scattered cases, it also diverts effort from developing more reliable methods, such as noncoercive expert interrogation, or effective control of WMD. It is not as though the stakes have been trivial until this moment in time. Over history, torture has been normatively rejected in the face of the prospect of eternal damnation, the imperatives of war and national survival, and the demands of solving or preventing other mass crimes. Modern nations, from Europe to Japan to Israel, beset by ruthless terrorism, have held back or been restrained from validating torture in the name of democratic values and human rights.

The world torture constructs is a world that rejects foundational principles of the legal order that protects human dignity.[20] If we are willing to torture putative terrorists, we can no longer assert the universality of rights and instead must divide the world into those entitled to full protection and those deemed too dangerous for such an entitlement. Nor should we expect reciprocity, not only from terrorists but from other nations who, following our lead, have gotten the habit of torturing their most feared enemies. This is more like the Dark Ages than a new world.

We are not there yet. The formal condemnations of torture, the rescinding of the worst memorandum, the prosecution of the lowest level, and the arguments framed in terms of limited or regulated torture all speak to an uncomfortable recognition that much hinges on our recognition of the norm. But the exemption of leaders from consequence belies this grudging recognition. If we fail to act on what we know, are we also complicit in the next recurrence of such inhumanity?

15

TORTURE IN U.S. PRISONS

Jamie Fellner

Jamie Fellner is the director of Human Rights Watch's United States program, where she has spotlighted conditions in U.S. prisons and the human rights implications of U.S. national and international security policies. This piece looks at torture and cruel, inhumane, and degrading treatment in U.S. prisons today.

Everyone familiar with U.S. jails and prisons knows cruel, inhumane, and degrading treatment and even torture can be part of inmate life behind bars. Such abuses are in part a reflection of the dehumanizing culture of corrections, a culture whose worst tendencies are exacerbated by overcrowding, tight budgets, and the public's belief that punishment—i.e., the infliction of misery—is the primary purpose of imprisonment. When it occurs, frequent abuse is also, however, a sign of management failure—a failure of will, leadership, and commitment to safe and humane confinement.

Inmates in American prisons and jails are not routinely and systematically mistreated, but acts of brutality are far from rare. In recent years, inmates have been beaten with fists and batons, stomped, kicked, shot; they have had their hands and arms twisted painfully, their ears boxed; they have been choked, slammed against walls, slammed face-first onto concrete floors, shocked multiple times by stun devices and sprayed repeatedly in the face with chemical sprays. Inmates have ended up with broken noses, missing teeth, broken jaws, smashed ribs, perforated eardrums, burn scars—not to mention psychological scars and emotional pain. Some have died.

Both men and women prisoners also face staff rape and sexual abuse from staff and other prisoners. Correctional officers will bribe, coerce, or violently force inmates into vaginal, anal, and oral sex. Prison staff have laughed at and ignored the pleas of male prisoners seeking protection from rape by other inmates.

There are no national or even state-specific statistics on this kind of staff abuse of inmates. Prison systems have little incentive to gather such statistics, and no laws require them to do so. The incidents we know about—from litigation, newspaper stories, investigations by special commissions and human rights groups—constitute the tip of the iceberg. But the truth is, we do not know how big that iceberg is.

Sometimes abuse becomes rampant in individual prisons. California's Pelican Bay State Prison during the 1990s is a notorious example of a facility rife with staff violence (and many California prisons and youth facilities to this day have serious abuse problems). In the worst cases, an entire prison system is fraught with abuse. In 1999, for example, a federal judge found a "culture of sadistic and malicious violence" through the Texas prison system.

Americans have a couple of misconceptions about torture that blind them to the significance of what is happening in U.S. prisons. First, they think that as a matter of definition torture involves mistreatment aimed at getting information or confessions from the victim. In fact, as discussed elsewhere in this volume, torture cannot be defined nearly so narrowly.

Second, Americans think the only prohibited mistreatment is torture, understood as the deliberate infliction of excruciating pain through horrific methods—e.g., electric shocks to the genitals. In fact, torture is part of a continuum of prohibited conduct that clearly includes more mundane methods—e.g., beatings—which may inflict physical or mental pain or suffering that is notable but not unbearable. The mistreatment inflicted on inmates in prison as punishment, retaliation, or intimidation falls within the international human rights prohibitions against torture and other cruel, inhumane, and degrading treatment or punishment.

There are two basic categories of inmate abuse in prisons: treatment that is sanctioned by express policy—i.e., those that correctional officials do not recognize as abusive—and conduct that violates prison policy, and is not formally authorized. A prime example of the mistreatment of inmates authorized by policy is the prolonged confinement of mentally ill prisoners in solitary confinement (called administrative or disciplinary segregation by prison officials). But because of the particular vulnerabilities and needs that accompany serious mental illness, months or years in isolation can produce intense psychological misery and even psychiatric breakdowns.

Prolonged supermaximum security confinement can violate international human rights standards even for inmates who are not mentally ill. More than twenty thousand prisoners in the United States spend their waking and sleeping hours locked in small, sometimes windowless cells sealed with solid or perforated steel doors. A few times a week they are let out of their cells for showers and solitary exercise in a small enclosed space, typically devoid of equipment. They have almost no access to educational or vocational activities or other sources of mental stimulation; they have scant opportunities for human interaction with anyone; they are handcuffed, shackled, and escorted by correctional officers every time they leave their cells. These conditions are unduly severe and disproportionate to legitimate security and inmate management objectives; they impose pointless suffering and humiliation; and they reflect a stunning disregard for the fact that all prisoners must have their dignity as humans respected, even prisoners who break the rules.

At the other end of the continuum, examples of authorized forms of degradation include various policies of the Maricopa County Jail in Arizona. These policies have included, for example, forcing male inmates to wear pink underwear and, for a while, permitting live webcast pictures of female inmates in the holding cell, including shots of strip searches and women using the toilet. (The broadcasts ended up being copied onto web porn sites.)

Unauthorized abuse of inmates typically consists of the wrongful use of physical force. Prison staff are, of course, permitted to use physical force to ensure safety and security within a facility. But they are permitted to use force only as a last resort and then are permitted to use only as much force as is necessary in a good-faith effort to restore order. Force cannot be used as punishment or to retaliate. Yet across the country there are constant incidents of staff who maliciously or sadistically use force for just such purposes. They either use physical force when none is needed, or they use far more force than is required in a given situation. Examples abound:

- The Department of Justice's inspector general recently reported on the abuse endured by Muslim men picked up after September 11, while detained at the federal Metropolitan Detention Center in Brooklyn, New York. For example, officers slammed unresisting, shackled inmates into walls and mocked them during body-cavity searches. A lawsuit by one of the detainees alleges that one of the officers pushed a pencil into the detainee's anus.

- Allen Donald Smith was arrested and held in a jail in Georgia. He and several other inmates wrote a letter to the county sheriff complaining about the filthy conditions in which they were held. In retaliation for this complaint, jail staff took Smith to a cell with a table in it on which another inmate was restrained facedown. Smith was forced to lie on his stomach on the dirty cell floor under the table, with his hands and feet cuffed to the table's legs. He was kept there for twenty-two hours and was not released to eat or go to the bathroom. He ultimately urinated and had to lie in his urine. When the inmate above him also urinated, that urine dripped down onto Smith.

• Sylvester Butler is a Florida prisoner with a history of psychiatric problems who is also borderline developmentally disabled. During a one-year period, corrections officers doused him with pepper spray and tear gas on at least seventeen occasions. They allege he was being disruptive and unruly, although each time he was sprayed, it was while he was confined in his cell. One spraying left him with second-degree burns on his shoulder and upper back. Another spraying was so extensive—and he was not taken to a shower to wash it off as required by policy—that his hip and upper buttocks developed large blisters; when they broke, the skin peeled off, leaving a large raw seeping wound. Another Florida prisoner, Curt Massie, suffered second-degree burns on his left arm, leg, back, and hip when he was sprayed for having made a funny face behind a nurse's back. Butler and Massie are plaintiffs in a class-action lawsuit alleging a system-wide pattern of malicious use of pepper spray to retaliate against annoying inmates.

• In January 2004, a videotape at a California facility captured two officers beating and kicking two inmates. One officer struck an inmate approximately twenty times in the face; another officer is shown kicking a handcuffed inmate in the head.   •

• When Florida inmate Frank Valdez died in 1999, every rib in his body was broken, his corpse bore the imprint of boot marks, and his testicles were badly swollen. Correctional officers admitted having struggled with him but denied they had used excessive force. They claimed most of his injuries had been "self-inflicted."

Inmate-on-inmate violence also remains a serious problem in U.S. prisons, and no doubt accounts for more injuries than staff violence.

One in ten state prisoners goes to a medical clinic for treatment because of injuries from a fight or assault. When staff are deliberately indifferent to inmate violence—and worse, when they facilitate or encourage it—they become complicit in torture or cruel mistreatment. Some inmates (primarily male) endure vicious and repeated rape by other inmates—while prison staff shrug their shoulders and ignore their pleas for protection. For example, between 2000 and 2002, Rodney Jonson, a black gay man imprisoned in Texas, was routinely bought and sold as a sex slave by prison gangs, raped and degraded almost daily, and threatened with death if he resisted. Prison officials refused to take his complaints seriously and would not put him in protective custody. They told him he must either "fight or fuck." There have also been cases in which staff deliberately place a disliked inmate in a cell with another inmate whom they expect—and want—to brutalize or rape him.

Even detained children and youth are not safe from staff brutality and abuse. They too are kicked, beaten, punched, choked, and sexually preyed upon by adult staff. The Maryland State Police recently filed criminal assault charges against staff at a youth facility in Maryland because of an incident in which one guard restrained a youth while three others kicked him and punched him in the face. In January 2004, the U.S. Department of Justice reported on terrible conditions at Arizona's juvenile detention centers, including sexual abuse of the children by staff members (and fellow inmates) that occurred "with disturbing frequency" and a level of physical abuse that was "equally disturbing."

Why Prisoners Are Abused

Most correctional officers are decent human beings who do not engage in flagrant inmate abuse. Of course, there are also officers who lack the appropriate values, temperament, self-control and professionalism. Given near total power over confined individuals, minimal opportunities for job satisfaction, and scant respect from the public, these officers can descend into sporadic or continual mistreatment of inmates. But the explanation that the abuse of prisoners is only the work of a few rogue officers is untenable. Responsibility for what happens within prisons lies with management. Staff violence and degradation of inmates (as well as inmate-on-inmate violence) reflects management failure.

Prison systems and individual prisons are hierarchical, quasimilitaristic organizations with clear chains of command. The single most important determinant of the institutional culture within a given prison system is the senior management, starting with the person at the top. In case after case in which violent staff have run amok in individual prisons or prison systems, one finds a warden or correctional director who has failed to establish—and enforce—clear policies and expectations about how staff will treat inmates. They have failed to establish—and communicate continually and unequivocally—a zero-tolerance policy for abuse.

The "default" culture in a prison is toxic. That is, the culture does not come automatically with respect for inmates as individuals with dignity and rights, or with a commitment that prison be as productive an experience as possible. Line staff face the continual temptations that come with wielding great power over individuals confined against their will. These temptations are enhanced if correctional officers despise, resent, and fear the inmates and if, as is so often the case today because of budget cuts, the lack of productive activities for the inmates generates even greater dynamics of ill will and hostility. If the default toxic culture is to be overcome, senior management must exercise strong leadership. Unfortunately, some do not.

As Martin Horn, head of the New York City jail system has said, "If the [prison] culture is one that values human life, one that respects the individual and the rule of law and is based on integrity, the outcomes will be substantially different than if the culture devalues the individual.

Only leaders can create such an atmosphere and that is ultimately their most important task." [1]

A culture of respect for inmates in which abuse is rare requires careful staff training, constant supervision, effective and fair staff disciplinary procedures, reflection of values in all institutional policies and pronouncements, oversight, and transparency. It is a rare prison system that has all or even most of these ingredients.

Staff must be recruited and trained to serve the purpose of rebuilding lives as well as protecting the community. Yet because of budget pressures as well as management inattention, we find careless recruitment and inadequate training of line staff. Academic or professional requirements for the job are meager, consistent with low pay and low public regard for the job. Training of staff is limited at best and terrible at worst. It is particularly limited on such crucial matters as interpersonal skills, how to use force properly and to avoid excessive force, how to deal with difficult inmates and to de-escalate potential conflict situations, how to manage anger, and how to deal with the inevitable stress of the job. Staff receive little encouragement to develop positive values and attitudes toward their work and the inmates.

Management must set—and enforce—a zero-tolerance policy regarding staff abuse of prisoners. Good use of force policies are not enough. Management must monitor, supervise, and investigate continually and carefully to ensure those policies are honored in practice. When senior officials maintain a "see no evil, hear no evil" approach to inmate complaints about violent staff or staff sexual relations with inmates, proliferating abuse is almost inevitable. Time and time again, when the history of violence in a prison is analyzed, one finds heedless senior management who were dismissive of inmate grievances, who did not insist on meaningful investigations into complaints, and who were far too quick to accept an officer's word against an inmate's. Senior officials did not use the available administrative and disciplinary mechanisms to make clear to all staff that anyone who engages in abuse—or who covers up such abuse—will be disciplined and/or the case will be turned over to a district attorney for possible criminal prosecution.

Finally, and worst of all, some senior officials expressly or tacitly condone the abuse of inmates. They accept it as a way to maintain control over prisoners, they shy away from taking on powerful prison-guard unions, and they feel no pressure from inside or outside the department to do anything about it. When a complaint comes to their attention, they signal to their staff—by a smile, by a shrug, by inaction—that abuse is simply not their problem. Confronting a stunning pattern of staff assaults, abusive use of electronic stun devices, beatings, and brutality at one California prison, a federal judge in *Madrid v. Gomez* concluded the violence "appears to be open, acknowledged, tolerated and sometimes expressly approved" by high-ranking corrections officials.

The potential for abuse is inherent in the very nature of incarceration, where staff exercise near total control over men and women who would rather be elsewhere. Correctional officers, the frontline staff who interact with prisoners daily, have a difficult job in the best of circumstances. But the best of circumstances do not exist today: working in insufficient numbers, prison officers are asked to exercise power over and maintain control of prisoners packed into greatly overcrowded facilities at a time when budgets for inmate services and programs have declined, leaving prisoners with few opportunities for productive and peaceful activities. Corrections officials have noted that as inmate programs are reduced, inmate tension and assaults on staff and one another increase. Prisons in which inmates are violent with one another and with staff are prisons with a high risk that staff will become excessively and unnecessarily violent with prisoners.

Prison abuse also reflects the absence of sufficient external pressure and scrutiny. The courts' ability to scrutinize prison conditions and protect prisoners has been weakened considerably by the Prison Litigation Reform Act of 1996, which makes it harder for prisoners to get into court, to find lawyers willing to take their cases, and to obtain meaningful remedies. Judicial relief is available only in the most egregious cases of widespread abuse. The Special Litigation Section of the Civil Rights Division of the Department of Justice does an excellent job of investigating prisons and uncovering patterns of egregious abuse, but it is too short-staffed to take on more than a handful of cases at any moment. External scrutiny is also limited by laws unduly restricting press access to prisoners, by the lack of independent agencies charged with monitoring the treatment of inmates, and by the difficulty that monitoring groups such as Human Rights Watch and Amnesty International have in gaining access to prisons. Absent independent monitors appointed after litigation, effective oversight of prisons or prison systems by impartial entities or experts is rare.

Many Americans believe that prisons should be miserable places because inmates are criminals. "If you can't do the time, don't do the crime," reflects a cavalier public approach to appalling prison conditions, putting the responsibility on the inmate for breaking the law, rather than on the public for ensuring that prison be humane. With rare exceptions—usually prompted by a scandal—politicians simply have not paid much attention to the nature of life behind bars—and neither politicians nor the public have given much thought to the question of what their huge prison investment will yield.

From a human rights perspective, the purpose of prison should never be simply punishment. Recognizing the inherent dignity of every human being means recognizing their potential for change, growth, redemption, rehabilitation. Human rights principles do not just prohibit torture or cruel, inhumane, or degrading treatment—they also mandate positive action. According to the International Covenant on Civil and Political Rights, the goal of imprisonment should be rehabilitation. Such a goal not only respects the rights of prisoners, it also furthers the community interest in safety and reduced crime.

If prisons were operated with a goal of rehabilitation—and if prison officials were held accountable for their ability to contribute to that goal—we would see far less mistreatment and abuse in prison. Prison staff would be hired, trained, and managed to view their interaction with prisoners as contributing to the improvement of inmate skills, attitude, and prospects for a successful reentry to the community. Senior prison officials would understand staff abuse of inmates as undermining and indeed contradicting the purpose of imprisonment. The public would view such abuse as, ultimately, endangering the community.

We are a long way from such a change in attitudes toward imprisonment. But there is reason for cautious optimism. The horrors of Abu Ghraib have sparked much-needed questions about conditions in U.S. prisons and the creation of a private blue-ribbon commission on prison violence. Highly publicized incidents of abuse in California and Massachussetts led to the creation of state commissions that have issued powerful blueprints for change. Rejecting the inevitability of prison rape and staff sexual abuse, Congress has put money and muscle behind efforts to prevent them.

Rehabilitation may be an unfashionable term, but it is inherent in the new focus on "reentry"—how to ensure the successful transition of 650,000 men and women every year from prison back to their communities. The public is finally beginning to realize that if prisons are destructive places, communities will suffer. Perhaps community self-interest will thus be the vehicle for establishing the internal controls and the external scrutiny needed to ensure that a sentence to prison is not a sentence to abuse.

16

JUSTIFYING TORTURE

Kenneth Roth

As executive director of Human Rights Watch, Kenneth Roth has conducted human rights investigations around the globe, devoting special attention to issues of justice and accountability for gross abuses of human rights, and standards governing military conduct in time of war. This piece examines why Washington's unique influence has made its undermining of the torture prohibition uniquely damaging.

In most cases, when a government breaches international human rights and humanitarian law, the breach is considered a violation. It is condemned or prosecuted, but the rule remains firm. Yet when a government as dominant and influential as the United States openly defies that law and seeks to justify its defiance by undermining the law itself, it invites others to do the same. The U.S. government's deliberate and continuing use of "coercive interrogation"—its acceptance and deployment of torture and other cruel, inhuman, or degrading treatment—has had this insidious effect, well beyond the consequences of an ordinary abuser. That unlawful conduct has also undermined Washington's much-needed credibility as a proponent of human rights and a leader in the campaign against terrorism.

This systematic and continuing use of coercive interrogation jeopardizes a pillar of international human rights law—a centuries-old proscription, reaffirmed unconditionally in numerous widely ratified human rights treaties. These treaties oblige governments never to subject detainees to torture—defined as the intentional infliction of severe pain or suffering—or other cruel, inhuman, or degrading treatment. As made clear in the Convention against Torture, which the United States ratified in 1994, "No exceptional circumstances whatsoever, whether a state of war or a threat of war, internal political instability or any other public emergency, may be invoked as a justification of torture." Yet in fighting terrorism, the Bush Administration has treated this cornerstone obligation as merely hortatory—a matter of choice, not duty.

This disdain for so fundamental a principle has done enormous damage to the global system for protecting human rights. Broad public condemnation has certainly greeted the U.S. government's use of torture and other abusive techniques. To some extent that outrage has reinforced the rules that Washington violated—but not enough. Washington's lawless example is so powerful, its influence so singular, that its deliberate breach threatens to overshadow the condemnations and leave human rights law significantly weakened. If even so basic a rule as the ban on torture can be flouted, other rights are inevitably undermined as well.

To make matters worse, the Bush Administration has developed outrageous legal theories to try to justify many of its coercive techniques, most notably in an August 2002 opinion issued by the Justice Department's Office of Legal Counsel. Whether defining torture so narrowly as to render its prohibition meaningless, suggesting bogus legal defenses for torturers, or claiming that the president has inherent power to order torture, the administration and its lawyers have directly challenged the absolute ban on abusing detainees. Even when the administration replaced that opinion with a new one, in December 2004, it never repudiated the claim that the president had the power to order torture, nor did it commit to abide by the parallel prohibition of cruel, inhuman, or degrading treatment.

The demonstration effect of the Bush Administration's use of torture and other abusive interrogation is compounded by the weakening of one of the most important governmental voices for human rights. Washington's record of promoting human rights has always been mixed. For every offender it berated for human rights transgressions, there was another whose abuses it ignored, excused, or even supported. Yet despite this inconsistency, the United States historically has played a key role in defending human rights. Its embrace of coercive interrogation—part of a broader betrayal of human rights principles in the name of combating terrorism—has significantly impaired its ability to mount that defense.

Governments facing human rights pressure from the United States now find it increasingly easy to turn the tables, to challenge Washington's standing to uphold principles that it itself violates. Whether it is Egypt defending torture by reference to U.S. practice, Malaysia justifying administrative detention by invoking Guantánamo, Russia citing Abu Ghraib to blame abuses in Chechnya solely on low-level soldiers, Nepal justifying a coup by reference to America's post–September 11 excesses, or Cuba claiming that the Bush Administration had "no moral authority to accuse" it of human rights violations, repressive governments find it easier to deflect U.S. pressure because of Washington's own sorry counterterrorism record on human rights. Indeed, when asked by Human Rights Watch to protest administrative detention in Malaysia and prolonged incommunicado detention in Uganda, State Department officials demurred, explaining, in the words of one, "with what we are doing in Guantánamo, we're on thin ice to push this." [1]

Similarly, many human rights defenders, particularly in the Middle East and North Africa, now cringe when the United States comes to their defense. Reformers in the Middle East speak of "the hug of death"—the ill effects of Washington's hypocritical embrace. They may crave a powerful ally, but identifying too closely with a government that so brazenly ignores international law—whether in Iraq or the campaign against terrorism—has become a sure route to disrepute. To his credit, President Bush, in a November 2003 speech, deplored "sixty years of Western nations excusing and accommodating the lack of freedom" in the Arab world. Recalling U.S. efforts to roll back communist dictatorships in Eastern Europe, President Bush committed the United States to a new "forward strategy of freedom." Yet because of animosity toward Washington's policies, the close collaboration with civil society that characterized U.S. prodemocracy efforts in Eastern Europe is now more difficult in the Middle East and North Africa. This animosity is not anti-Americanism, as it is often misconstrued in an effort to dismiss it, but anti–American policyism.

Washington's loss of credibility has not been for lack of rhetorical support for concepts that are closely related to human rights, but the embrace of explicit human rights language seems to have been calculatedly rare. As in his January 2005 inauguration speech, President Bush speaks often of his devotion to "freedom" and "liberty," his opposition to "tyranny" and "terrorism," but rarely his commitment to human rights. The distinction has enormous significance. It is one thing to pronounce oneself on the side of the "free," quite another to be bound by the full array of human rights standards that are the foundation of freedom. It is one thing to declare oneself opposed to terrorism, quite another to embrace the body of international human rights and humanitarian law that enshrines the values rejecting terrorism. This linguistic sleight of hand—this refusal to accept the legal obligations embraced by rights-respecting states—has facilitated Washington's use of coercive interrogation.

What has been particularly frustrating about Washington's disregard for international standards is how senseless, even counterproductive, it has been—especially in the Middle East and North Africa, where counterterrorism efforts have focused. Open and responsive political systems are the best way to encourage people to pursue their grievances peacefully. But when the most vocal governmental advocate of democracy deliberately violates human rights, it undermines democratically inclined reformers and strengthens the appeal of those who preach more radical visions.

Moreover, because deliberately attacking civilians is an affront to the most basic human rights values, an effective defense against terrorism requires not only traditional security measures but also reinforcement of a human rights culture. The communities that are most influential with potential terrorists must themselves be persuaded that violence against civilians is never justified, regardless of the cause. But when the United States disregards human rights, it undermines that human rights culture and thus sabotages one of the most important tools for dissuading potential terrorists. Instead, U.S. abuses have provided a new rallying cry for terrorist recruiters, and the pictures from Abu Ghraib have become the recruiting posters for Terrorism, Inc. Many militants need no additional incentive to attack civilians, but if a weakened human rights culture eases even a few fence-sitters toward the path of violence, the consequences could be dire.

And for what? To vent frustration, to exact revenge—perhaps, but not because torture and mistreatment are needed for protection. Respect for the Geneva Conventions does not preclude vigorously interrogating detainees about a limitless range of topics. The U.S. Army's interrogation manual makes clear that abuse undermines the quest for reliable information. The U.S. military command in Iraq says that Iraqi detainees are providing more useful intelligence when they are not subjected to coercion. In the words of Craig Murray, the United Kingdom's former ambassador to Uzbekistan, who was speaking of the U.K.'s reliance on torture-extracted testimony, "We are selling our souls for dross." [2]

Moreover, coercive interrogation is making us less safe by effectively precluding criminal prosecution of its victims. Once a confession is coerced, it becomes extremely difficult to prove, as due process requires, that a subsequent prosecution of the suspect is free of the fruits of that coercion. As a result, the Bush Administration finds itself holding some suspects who clearly have joined terrorist conspiracies and might have been criminally convicted and subjected to long prison terms, but against whom prosecution has become impossible. In February 2005, the Central Intelligence Agency began openly fretting about the problem. What happens, it worried, when continued detention without trial becomes politically impossible, but prosecution is legally impossible because the use of coercive interrogation has effectively precluded it?[3]

None of this is to say that the United States is the worst human rights abuser. Perusal of Human Rights Watch's annual *World Report* will show many more serious contenders for that notorious title. But the sad truth is that Washington's unmatched influence has made its contribution to the degradation of human rights standards unique.

It is not enough to argue, as its defenders do, that the Bush Administration is well intentioned—that it is the "good guys," in the words of the *Wall Street Journal*.[4] A society ordered on intentions rather than law is a lawless society. Nor does it excuse the administration's human rights record, as its defenders have tried to do, to note that it removed two tyrannical governments—the Taliban in Afghanistan and the Ba'ath Party in Iraq. Attacks on repressive regimes cannot justify attacks on the body of principles that makes their repression illegal.

To redeem its credibility as a proponent of human rights and an effective leader of the campaign against terrorism, the Bush Administration needs urgently to reaffirm its commitment to human rights. It should begin by ending its use of all forms of coercive interrogation.

Cover-Up and Self-Investigation

When the photos from Abu Ghraib became public, the Bush Administration reacted like many abusive governments that are caught red-handed: it went into damage-control mode. It agreed that the torture and abuse featured in the photographs were wrong, but sought to minimize the problem. The abusers, it claimed, were a handful of errant soldiers, a few "bad apples" at the bottom of the barrel. The problem, it argued, was contained, both geographically (one section of Abu Ghraib prison) and structurally (only low-level soldiers, not more senior commanders). The abuse photographed at Abu Ghraib and broadcast around the world, it maintained, had nothing to do with the decisions and policies of more senior officials. President Bush vowed that "wrongdoers will be brought to justice," but as of May 2005, virtually all of those facing prosecution were of the rank of sergeant or below.

Key to this damage control was a series of carefully limited investigations—at least ten so far. Most of the investigations, such as those conducted by Major General George Fay and Lieutenant General Anthony Jones, involved uniformed military officials examining the conduct of their subordinates; these officers lacked the authority to scrutinize senior Pentagon officials. The one investigation with the theoretical capacity to examine the conduct of Defense Secretary Donald Rumsfeld and his top aides—the inquiry led by former Defense Secretary James Schlesinger—was appointed by Rumsfeld himself and seemed to go out of its way to distance him from the problem. (At the press conference releasing the investigative report, Schlesinger said that Rumsfeld's resignation "would be a boon to all America's enemies.") The Schlesinger investigation lacked the independence of, for example, the September 11 Commission, which was established with the active involvement of the U.S. Congress. As for the Central Intelligence Agency—the branch of the U.S. government believed to hold the most important terrorist suspects—it has apparently escaped scrutiny by anyone other than its own inspector general. Meanwhile, no one seems to be looking at the role of President Bush and other senior administration officials.

When an unidentified government official retaliated against a critic of the Bush Administration by revealing his wife to be a CIA agent—a serious crime because it could endanger her—the administration agreed, under pressure, to appoint a special prosecutor who has been promised independence from administration direction. Yet the administration has refused to appoint a special prosecutor to determine whether senior officials authorized torture and other forms of coercive interrogation—a far more serious and systematic offense. As a result, no criminal inquiry that the administration does not itself control is being conducted into its abusive interrogation methods. The flurry of self-investigations cannot obscure the lack of any genuinely independent one.

The Policies Behind Abu Ghraib

What would a genuinely independent investigation find? It would reveal that the abuses of Abu Ghraib did not erupt spontaneously at the lowest levels of the military chain of command. They were not merely a "management" failure, as the Schlesinger investigation suggested. They were the direct product of an environment of lawlessness, an environment created by policy decisions taken at the highest levels of the Bush Administration, many long before the start of the Iraq war. They reflect a determination to fight terrorism unconstrained by fundamental principles of international human rights and humanitarian law—despite commitments by the United States and governments around the world to respect those principles even in time of war and severe security threats. The Bush Administration's decisions received important support in the United States from a chorus of partisan pundits and academics who, claiming that an unprecedented security threat justified unprecedented measures, were all too eager to abandon the fundamental principles on which their nation had been founded. Those decisions included:

- The decision not to grant the detainees in U.S. custody at Guantánamo their rights under the Geneva Conventions, even though the
conventions apply to all people picked up on the battlefield of
Afghanistan. Senior Bush officials vowed that all detainees would be
treated "humanely," but that vow seems never to have been seriously
implemented and at times was qualified (and arguably eviscerated) by
a self-created exception for "military necessity." Meanwhile, the effective shredding of the Geneva Conventions—and the correspon-
ding sidestepping of the U.S. Army's interrogation manual—sent U.S.
interrogators the signal that, in the words of one leading counterterrorist official, "the gloves came off."[5]
- The decision not to clarify for nearly two years that, regardless of the
applicability of the Geneva Conventions, all detainees in U.S. custody
are protected by the parallel requirements of the International
Covenant on Civil and Political Rights (ICCPR) and Convention
against Torture (CAT). Even when, at the urging of human rights
groups, a senior Pentagon official belatedly reaffirmed, in June 2003,
that the convention prohibited not only torture but also other forms
of ill treatment, that announcement was communicated to interrogators, if at all, in a way that had no discernible impact on their behavior.
- The decision to interpret the prohibition of cruel, inhuman, or degrading treatment narrowly, to permit certain forms of coercive interrogation—that is, certain efforts to ratchet up a suspect's pain,
suffering, and humiliation to make him talk. At the time of ratifying
the ICCPR in 1992 and CAT in 1994, the U.S. government said it
would interpret this prohibition to mean the same thing as the requirements of the Fifth, Eighth, and Fourteenth amendments to the
U.S. Constitution. The clear intent was to require that if an interrogation technique would be unconstitutional if used in an American
police station or jail, it would violate these treaties if used against sus-

pects overseas. Yet U.S. interrogators under the Bush Administration have routinely subjected overseas terrorist suspects to abusive techniques that would clearly have been prohibited if used in the United States. That the use of cruel, inhuman, or degrading treatment was intentional became clear during the confirmation process of Attorney General Alberto Gonzales. In his written reply to Senate questions, he interpreted the U.S. reservation as permitting the use of cruel, inhuman, or degrading treatment so long as it was done against non-Americans outside the United States—making the U.S. government the only government in the world to publicly claim as a matter of policy the power to use cruel, inhuman, or degrading treatment. For similar reasons, the Bush Administration in late 2004 successfully stopped a Congressional effort to proscribe the CIA's use of torture and inhumane treatment in interrogation.

- The decision to hold some suspects—eleven known and reportedly some three dozen—in unacknowledged incommunicado detention, beyond the reach of even the International Committee of the Red Cross. (Many other suspects were apparently temporarily hidden from the ICRC.) Victims of such "disappearances" are at the greatest risk of torture and other mistreatment. For example, U.S. forces continue to maintain closed detention sites in Afghanistan, where beatings, threats, and sexual humiliation are still reported. At least twenty-six prisoners have died in American custody in Iraq and Afghanistan since 2002 in what Army and Navy investigators have concluded or suspect were acts of criminal homicide. One of those deaths happened as recently as September 2004.

- The refusal for more than two years to prosecute U.S. soldiers implicated in the deaths of two suspects in U.S. custody in Afghanistan—deaths ruled "homicides" by U.S. Army pathologists. Instead, the interrogators were reportedly sent to Iraq, where some were allegedly involved in more abuse.

- The approval by Defense Secretary Rumsfeld of some interrogation methods for Guantánamo that violated, at the very least, the prohibition of cruel, inhuman, or degrading treatment and possibly the ban on torture. These techniques included placing detainees in painful stress positions, hooding them, stripping them of their clothes, and scaring them with guard dogs. That approval was later rescinded, but it contributed to the environment in which America's legal obligations were seen as dispensable.

- The reported approval by an unidentified senior Bush Administration official, and use, of "waterboarding"—known as the "submarine" in Latin America—a torture technique in which the victim is made to believe he will drown, and in practice sometimes does. Remarkably, Porter Goss, the CIA director, defended waterboarding in March 2005 testimony before the Senate as a "professional interrogation technique." [6]

- The sending of suspects to governments such as Syria, Uzbekistan, and Egypt that practice systematic torture. Sometimes diplomatic assurances have been sought that the suspects would not be mistreated, but if, as in these cases, the government receiving the suspect routinely flouts its legal obligation under the Convention against Torture, it was wrong to expect better compliance with the nonbinding word of a diplomat. The administration claimed that it monitored prisoners' treatment, but a single prisoner has none of the anonymity afforded by a larger group and would be unable to report abuse for fear of reprisal. One U.S. official who visited foreign detention sites disparaged this charade: "They say they are not abusing them, and that satisfies the legal requirement, but we all know they do." [7]

- The decision (adopted from the Bush Administration's earliest days) to oppose and undermine the International Criminal Court, in part out of fear that it might compel the United States to prosecute U.S. personnel implicated in war crimes or other comparable offenses that the administration would prefer to ignore. That signaled a determination to protect U.S. personnel from external accountability for human rights offenses that the U.S. government might authorize.

- The decision by the Justice Department, the Defense Department, and the White House counsel to concoct dubious legal theories to justify torture. Despite objections from the State Department and professional military attorneys, these government departments, under the direction of politically appointed lawyers, offered such absurd interpretations of the law as that President Bush has "commander-in-chief authority" to order torture. By that theory, Slobodan Milosevic and Saddam Hussein may as well be given the keys to their jail cells, since they, too, presumably would have had "commander-in-chief authority" to authorize the atrocities they directed. The Justice Department, in a December 2004 memorandum modifying certain of these legal theories, chose not to repudiate this radical claim, but instead said that repudiation was unnecessary because the president opposes torture.

These policy decisions, made not by low-level soldiers but by senior officials of the Bush Administration, created an "anything goes" atmosphere, an environment in which the ends were assumed to justify the means. Sometimes the mistreatment of detainees was merely tolerated, other times it was actively encouraged or even ordered. In that environment, when the demand came from on high for "actionable intelligence"—intelligence that would help respond to the steady stream of U.S. casualties at the hands of Iraqi insurgents—it was hardly surprising that interrogators saw no obstacle in the legal prohibition of torture and mistreatment.

To this day, the Bush Administration has failed to repudiate many of these decisions. It continues to refuse to apply the Geneva Conventions to any of the more than five hundred detainees held at Guantánamo (despite a U.S. court ruling rejecting its position) and to many others detained in Iraq and Afghanistan. It continues to "disappear" detainees, despite ample proof that these "ghost detainees" are extraordinarily vulnerable to torture. It refuses to disown the practice of "rendering" suspects to governments that torture. It refuses to accept the global duty never to use cruel, inhuman, or degrading treatment. It continues its vendetta against the International Criminal Court. It has only selectively repudiated the many specious arguments for torture contained in the administration lawyers' notorious "torture memos." For these reasons, the Bush Administration reportedly continued as late as June 2004—long after the Abu Ghraib mistreatment became public—to subject Guantánamo detainees to beatings, prolonged isolation, sexual humiliation, extreme temperatures, and painful stress positioning—practices that the International Committee of the Red Cross reportedly called "tantamount to torture." [8]

As he picked his cabinet for his second presidential term, President Bush seemed to rule out even informal accountability. Secretary of State Colin Powell, the cabinet official who most forcefully opposed the administration's disavowal of the Geneva Conventions, left his post. Defense Secretary Donald Rumsfeld, who ordered abusive interrogation techniques in violation of international law, stayed on. White House Counsel Alberto Gonzales, who sought production of the memos justifying torture and who wrote that the fight against terrorism renders "obsolete" and "quaint" the Geneva Conventions' limitations on the interrogation and treatment of prisoners, was rewarded with appointment as attorney general. [9] As for the broader Bush Administration, the November 2004 electoral victory seems to have reinforced its traditional disinclination to serious self-examination. It persists in its refusal to admit any role in Abu Ghraib and other interrogation abuses.

The Twisted Logic of Torture

A warped and dangerous logic lies behind the Bush Administration's refusal to reject coercive interrogation. Many American security officials seem to believe that such interrogation is necessary to protect Americans and their allies from a catastrophic terrorist attack. Torture and inhumane treatment may be wrong, they contend, but mass murder is worse, so the lesser evil must be tolerated to prevent the greater one. Yet, aware of how fundamental the prohibition of torture is to modern civilization, even proponents of a hard-line approach to counterterrorism are reluctant to prescribe systematic torture. Instead, they purport to create a rare exception to the rule against torture by invoking the "ticking bomb" scenario, a situation in which interrogators are said to learn that a terrorist suspect in custody knows where a ticking bomb has been planted and must urgently force that information from him to save lives.

The ticking-bomb scenario makes for great philosophical discussion, but it rarely arises in real life—at least not in a way that avoids opening the door to pervasive torture. In fact, interrogators hardly ever learn that a suspect in custody knows of a particular, imminent terrorist bombing. Intelligence is rarely if ever good enough to provide such specific advance warning, let alone to demonstrate a particular suspect's knowledge of an imminent attack. Instead, interrogators tend to use circumstantial evidence to demonstrate such "knowledge," such as someone's association with or presumed membership in a terrorist group. Moreover, the ticking-bomb scenario is a dangerously expansive metaphor capable of embracing anyone who might have knowledge not just of immediate attacks but also of attacks at unspecified times in the future. After all, why are the victims of only an imminent terrorist attack deserving of protection by torture? Why not also use torture to prevent a terrorist attack tomorrow or next week or next year? And

once the taboo against torture is broken, why stop with the alleged terrorists themselves? Why not also torture their families or associates—
anyone who might provide life-saving information? The slope is very
slippery.

Israel provides an instructive example of how dangerously elastic the
ticking-bomb rationale can become. In 1987, the Landau Commission
in Israel authorized the use of "moderate physical pressure" in ticking-
bomb situations. A practice initially justified as rare and exceptional,
taken only when necessary to save lives, gradually became standard procedure. Soon, some 80 to 90 percent of Palestinian security detainees
were being tortured—until, in 1999, the Israeli Supreme Court cur-
tailed the practice. The rapid acceleration of the use of torture during
Argentina's "dirty war" provides another example of how difficult it is
to limit torture once the door to its use is opened.

Other schemes have also been suggested to allow only exceptional
torture. Judges might be asked to approve any use of torture. Consent of
the highest levels of the executive branch might be required. Yet in the
end, any effort to regulate torture ends up legitimizing it and inviting its
repetition. "Never" cannot be redeemed if allowed to be read as "sometimes." Regulation too easily becomes license.

The Bush Administration tried to allow just limited coercion
through tight rules, but that, predictably, led to more expansive use.
Once a government allows interrogators to ratchet up the level of pain,
suffering, and humiliation, severe abuse will not be far behind. That's
because a hardened terrorist is unlikely to be moved by minor discomfort or modest levels of pain. Once coercion is permitted, interrogators
will be tempted to intensify the mistreatment until the suspect cracks.
And so, mere coercion gives way to cruel, inhuman, or degrading treatment, which in turn gives way to torture.

As most professional interrogators explain, and as the U.S. Army's interrogation manual confirms, coercive interrogation is far less likely to

produce reliable information than the time-tested methods of careful questioning, probing, cross-checking, and gaining the confidence of the detainee. A person facing severe pain is likely to say whatever he thinks will stop the torture. But a skilled interrogator can often extract accurate information from the toughest suspect without resorting to coercion.

Moreover, once the norm against torture is breached, it is difficult to limit the consequences. Those who face increased risk of torture are not only "terrorist suspects" but anyone who finds himself in custody anywhere in the world—including, of course, Americans. After all, how can the United States protest others' mistreatment of its troops when their jailors do no more than what Washington does to its own detainees?

What's more, using torture and mistreatment has dangerous implications for the campaign against terrorism. Why, after all, is it acceptable to breach the fundamental prohibition of torture but not acceptable to breach the fundamental prohibition against attacking civilians? The torturer may justify his conduct by appeal to a higher good, but so do most terrorists. In neither case should the end be allowed to justify the means.

The European Union

As U.S. credibility on human rights wanes, there is an urgent need for others to assume the mantle of leadership. The European Union is an obvious candidate, but its performance has been inconsistent at best. At a formal level, the E.U. believes that "establishing the rule of law and protecting human rights are the best means of strengthening the international order." It has also repeatedly affirmed that all measures against terrorism must comply fully with international human rights and humanitarian law. And it has been a firm supporter of the emerging international system of justice.

Yet European governments themselves have been complicit in torture. Sweden, for example, sent two terrorist suspects to Egypt, a government with an established record of systematic torture. Stockholm tried to hide behind the fig leaf of diplomatic assurances from Cairo that the men would not be mistreated, but those assurances were predictably ignored. Germany, the Netherlands, Austria, and the United Kingdom have also returned or attempted to return terrorist or security suspects to places where they were at risk of torture. The United Kingdom refuses to rule out using information extracted from torture in court proceedings; its fig leaf is that it does not commission the torture itself, but merely passively receives its fruits, even though its ongoing relationship with intelligence partners ends up encouraging more torture.

These abusive practices compromise the European Union's ability to fill the leadership void left by Washington's embrace of coercive interrogation. At a moment that calls for distance from misguided American practices, the European Union seems to be toying with emulation. A clear recommitment to human rights principle is immediately needed if the European Union is to serve as an effective counterweight to Washington's insidious influence on human rights standards.

The Way Forward

Faced with substantial evidence showing that the abuses at Abu Ghraib and elsewhere were caused in large part by official government policies, the Bush Administration must reaffirm the importance of making human rights a guiding force for U.S. conduct, even in fighting terrorism. That requires acknowledging and reversing the policy decisions behind the administration's torture and mistreatment of detainees, holding accountable those responsible at all levels of government for this abuse (not just a bunch of privates and sergeants), and publicly committing to ending all forms of coercive interrogation. These steps are necessary to reaffirm the prohibition of torture and ill treatment, to redeem

Washington's voice as a credible proponent of human rights, and to restore the effectiveness of a U.S.–led campaign against terrorism.

Yet all that is easier said than done. How can President Bush and the Republican-controlled U.S. Congress be convinced to establish a fully independent investigative commission—similar to the one created to examine the attacks of September 11, 2001—to determine what went wrong in the administration's interrogation practices and to prescribe remedial steps? How can Attorney General Gonzales, who as White House counsel played a central role in formulating the administration's interrogation policy, be persuaded to recognize his obvious conflict of interest and appoint a special prosecutor charged with investigating criminal misconduct independently of the Justice Department's direction? These are not steps that the administration or its congressional allies will take willingly. Pressure will be needed.

And that pressure cannot and should not come only from the usual suspects. The torture and abuse of prisoners is an affront to the most basic American values. It is antithetical to the core beliefs in the integrity of the individual on which the United States was founded. And it violates one of the most basic prohibitions of international law—a prohibition so fundamental that its breach is considered a crime of universal jurisdiction, prosecutable in any competent court worldwide.

This is not a partisan concern, not an issue limited to one part of the political spectrum. It is a matter that all Americans, and their friends around the world, should insist be meaningfully addressed and changed. If this fundamental right is not vindicated, it risks rocking the foundation on which all of our rights rest. There is no more important rights violation facing Americans today.

Acknowledgments

To New Press Executive Director Diane Wachtell and editorial assistant Joel Ariaratnam—who were full partners in this project from its genesis—production editor Sarah Fan, and copy editor Liz Polizzi for their patience, their persistence, and their confidence.

To Amy Bernstein, who provided invaluable contributions, including her inspiration in helping to get the project off the ground, her editing skills, and her collaboration on Héctor Timerman, Mary Fabri, and Sir Nigel Rodley's key contributions to this volume. To Professor Max du Plessis, who made important contributions to Cherie Booth's chapter on sexual violence and torture. To Margaret McCabe for wise counsel.

To Human Rights Watch staff, including Michael Bochenek, Meg Davis, Rachel Denber, Allison Gill, Jeri Laber, Lance Lattig, Scott Long, Joanne Mariner, Jean-Paul Marthoz, Jemera Rone, Acacia Shields, Mickey Spiegel, Jonathan Sugden, Peter Takirambudde, and José Miguel Vivanco for expertise on global torture practices. To Laura Boardman, Steve Crawshaw, Jennifer Gaboury, Miriam Mahlow, Kay Seok, Cara Shiel, and Tim Sowula for editing and other key assistance. To Elijah Zarwan, for his pitch-perfect translation of Marie-Monique Robin's chapter from French into English. To Minky Worden's husband, Gordon Crovitz, and baby Jack for missed dinners and too many torture discussions.

To torture victims and their families worldwide who have shared their experiences with Human Rights Watch, with the hope others will not suffer as they did.

Notes

1. *A History of Torture* James Ross

1. Demosthenes 30.37, quoted in Page duBois, *Torture and Truth* (New York: Routledge, 1991), pp. 49–50.
2. Aristotle, *Rhetoric* 1376b–1377a, quoted in duBois, *Torture and Truth,* p. 67.
3. *Digest* of Justinian, 48.18.1; 23, quoted in Malise Ruthven, *Torture: The Grand Conspiracy* (London: Weidenfeld & Nicolson, 1978), p. 31.
4. Edward Peters, *Torture* (Philadelphia: University of Pennsylvania Press, 1996, expanded edition), p. 35.
5. See Ruthven, *Torture,* p. 43.
6. See Harold Berman, *Law and Revolution* (Cambridge, MA: Harvard University Press, 1983).
7. Philippe Wielant, *Practijke Criminele,* quoted in Harold Rudolph, *Security, Terrorism and Torture* (Cape Town: Juta & Co., 1984), p. 161.
8. Johannes Voet, *Commentary on the Digests of Justinian,* quoted in Rudolph, *Security, Terrorism and Torture,* p. 227.
9. Joost Damhouder, *Praxis Rerum Criminalium,* chap 17, quoted in Ruthven, *Torture,* p. 64.
10. Antonius Matthaeus II, *Commentarius de Criminibus,* cited in Rudolph, *Security, Terrorism and Torture,* p. 163.
11. However, as in the rest of Europe, torture applied as a form of punishment persisted into the nineteenth century.
12. See H.C. Lea, *Materials Towards a History of Witchcraft* (Philadelphia: University of Pennsylvania Press, 1939), p. 554, cited in Ruthven, *Torture,* pp. 128–29.
13. See Lea, *Materials Towards a History of Witchcraft,* pp. 524–25, cited in Ruthven, *Torture,* p. 135.

14. See Lea, *Materials Towards a History of Witchcraft*, p. 710, cited in Ruthven, *Torture*, p. 139.

15. Ruthven, *Torture*, p. 12.

16. Lieber Code (1863), article 16.

17. N. Robinson, *The Universal Declaration of Human Rights* (1958), p. 108, cited in Nigel Rodley, *The Treatment of Prisoners Under International Law* (New York: Oxford University Press, 1999), p. 18.

18. Common Article 3 to the four Geneva Conventions of 1949.

19. International Covenant on Civil and Political Rights, articles 4 and 7.

20. Convention against Torture and Other Cruel, Inhuman or Degrading Treatment or Punishment, Article 2.

21. James Fitzjames Stephen, *A History of the Criminal Law of England* (London: MacMillan, 1883), vol. 1, p. 442, n. 1, cited in Malcolm Evans and Rod Morgan, *Preventing Torture* (Oxford: Clarendon Press, 1998), p. 7.

2. *Moral Prohibition at a Price* Michael Ignatieff

1. Mark Bowden, "The Dark Art of Interrogation," *Atlantic Monthly*, October 2003, p. 70.

2. As quoted in Sanford Levinson, ed., *Torture: A Collection* (New York: Oxford University Press, 2004), p. 24.

3. Ibid., p. 29, my emphasis.

4. Ibid.

5. *Ireland v. United Kingdom* (1978), 2 *European Human Rights Reports* 25; see also Fionnuala Ni Aolain, "The European Convention on Human Rights and Its Prohibition on Torture," in Levinson, *Torture*, pp. 213–27.

6. "Judgment Concerning the Legality of the General Security Service's Interrogation Methods" (1999), in Levinson, *Torture*, pp. 165–82.

7. Kenneth Roth, "Darfur and Abu Ghraib," *Human Rights Watch World Report 2005* (New York: Human Rights Watch, 2005), introduction.

8. Richard Posner, "Torture, Terrorism and Interrogation," in Levinson, *Torture*, p. 291.

9. Jean Bethke Elshtain, "Reflection on the Problem of 'Dirty Hands,' " in Levinson, *Torture*, p. 86.

10. Quoted in Levinson, *Torture*, p. 28, from John Conroy, *Unspeakable Acts, Ordinary People: the Dynamics of Torture* (New York: Knopf, 2000), p. 34.

11. See also Michael Walzer, "Political Action: The Problem of Dirty Hands," in Levinson,

Torture, pp. 61–77; also my own *The Lesser Evil: Political Ethics in an Age of Terror* (Princeton: Princeton University Press, 2004).

12. Alan Dershowitz, *Why Terrorism Works* (New Haven, CT: Yale University Press, 2002), pp. 131–64.

13. Ignatieff, *Lesser Evil*, pp. 136–44.

14. "Psychology and Sometimes a Slap: The Man Who Made Prisoners Talk," *New York Times*, December 12, 2004.

3. *Torture and Terrorism: Painful Lessons from Israel* Eitan Felner

1. William J. Brennan, "The Quest to Develop a Jurisprudence of Civil Liberties in Times of Security Crisis," a paper delivered in a symposium at Hebrew University, Jerusalem, December 22, 1987, pp. 13–14.

2. Alan Dershowitz has been the most outspoken advocate for legalizing torture in the United States since September 11. See Dershowitz, "Let America Take Its Cues from Israel Regarding Torture," *Jewish World Review*, January 30, 2002; Dershowitz, "Should the Ticking Bomb Terrorist Be Tortured? A Case Study in How a Democracy Should Make Tragic Choices," in *Why Terrorism Works* (New Haven: Yale University Press, 2002), chap. 4.

3. The Landau Commission also offered a legal justification for the use of force in such circumstances. According to the Commission, the "defense of necessity," found in Israel Penal Code was the legal basis for the use of force by GSS interrogators. This was harshly criticized by several legal experts. For a legal analysis of the Landau Report, see Mordechai Kremnitzer, "The Landau Commission Report—Was the Security Service Subordinated to the Law, or the Law to the 'Needs' of the Security Service?" 23(2–3) *Israel Law Review* 216 (1989), and other articles in that special issue of the *Israel Law Review* devoted to the Landau Report.

4. Ibid., sec. 3.16.

5. Daniel Statman, "The Question of Absolute Morality Regarding the Prohibition on Torture," 4 *Mishpat U-Mimshal* [Law & Government in Israel (1997)], p. 173. Translated from Hebrew and quoted by Emanuel Gross, "Symposium: Terrorism and the Law: Democracy in the War Against Terrorism—the Israeli Experience," 35 *Loyola of Los Angeles Law Review*, June 2002, fn 35. See also Mordechai Kremnitzer and Re'em Segev, "The Legality of Interrogational Torture: A Question of Proper Authorization or a Substantive Moral Issue?" 34 *Israel Law Review*, Fall 2000, p. 27.

6. Michael Gross, "Just and Jewish Warfare—Israeli Soldiers Seem to Disregard Rules of War," *Tikkun*, September 2001, available at http://www.findarticles.com/p/articles/mi_m1548/is_5_16/ai_78237512.

7. Henry Shue, "Torture," *Philosophy and Public Affairs* 7, no. 2 (Winter 1978), p. 143. See also Peter Singer, "Unspeakable Acts," *New York Review of Books,* February 27, 1986, and W.L. Twining and P.E. Twining, "Bentham on Torture," *Northern Ireland Legal Quarterly,* Autumn 1973, pp. 348–49.

8. Landau Commission Report, sec. 3.15.

9. *HCJ on GSS Interrogations,* hearing on May 20, 1998, Protocol, p. 5 (my emphasis).

10. A similar case appears at Michael Moore, "Torture and the Balance of Evils," 23(2–3) *Israel Law Review* (1989), pp. 291–92.

11. Landau Commission Report, sec. 4.2.

12. See U.S. Department of Justice, Office of Legal Counsel, "Memorandum for Alberto R. Gonzales, Counsel to the President," August 1, 2002, available at http://www.washingtonpost.com/wp-srv/nation/documents/dojinterrogationmemo20020801.pdf); U.S. Department of Justice, "Working Group Report Detainee Interrogations in the Global War on Terrorism: Assessment of Legal, Historical, Policy, and Operational Considerations," April 4, 2003, available at http://www2.gwu.edu/~nsarchiv/NSAEBB/NSAEBB127/03.04.04.pdf.

13. "Report of the Special Rapporteur on Torture and Other Cruel, Inhuman or Degrading Treatment or Punishment," para. 121.

14. Ari Shavit, "Judgment Day—Israel Facing Apocalypse," *Ha'aretz,* October 6, 2000.

15. "Bomb on Bus Kills 20 in Tel Aviv; Rabin Vows Action Against Palestinian Group Claiming Responsibility," *Washington Post,* October 20, 1994.

16. Quoted in *Ha'aretz,* July 30, 1995.

17. See, for example, B'Tselem, *Detention and Interrogation of Salem and Hanan "Ali," Husband and Wife, Residents of Bani Na'im Village,* June 1995.

18. Yuval Ginbar, *Routine Torture: Interrogation Methods of the General Security Service,* B'Tselem comprehensive report, February 1998.

19. For a more detailed discussion of the failure of the monitoring mechanisms to prevent the routine use of torture and bring to justice GSS perpetrators who went beyond the methods allowed by the Landau Commission, see *Legislation Allowing the Use of Physical Force and Mental Coercion in Interrogations by the General Security Service,* p. 37ff.

20. See Yuval Ginbar, "Legitimizing Torture: The Israeli High Court of Justice Rulings in

the Bilbeisi, Hamdan, and Mubarak Cases—An Annotated Sourcebook," B'Tselem special report, January 1997.

21. For instance, human rights organizations distributed a critical analysis made by B'Tselem of the ruling by the Israeli Supreme Court on the issue of torture to Supreme Court justices from other countries, urging them to discuss the issues raised in those rulings with their peers from the Israeli Court. They also distributed the report when Justices from the Court, notably the Supreme Court president, Justice Aaron Barak, gave public talks.

22. But the ruling fell short of outlawing torture or ill-treatment in all circumstances. The attorney general can still decide not to prosecute an interrogator faced with a "ticking bomb" situation. The Court also left open the possibility for the Knesset to pass legislation to make torture and ill-treatment legal. For a critical analysis of these loopholes, see "The Legality of Interrogational Torture."

23. Twining and Twining, "Bentham on Torture," pp. 348–49.

5. *Torture in Latin America* Juan E. Méndez

1. Under the Argentine dictatorship and in the years of transition to democracy, one human rights leader, Emilio Fermin Mignone, epitomized this selfless struggle. Mignone, whose daughter Mónica was taken from his house when she was twenty-four and is still counted among the "disappeared," was the founder of the Centro de Estudios Legales y Sociales (CELS), one of the most effective human rights organizations in the region. For a sample of Mignone's work to denounce and abolish torture, see his *Witness to the Truth* (Maryknoll, NY: Orbis, 1988) first published in Spanish as *Iglesia y Dictadura* (Buenos Aires: Ediciones del Pensamiento Nacional, 1986).

2. In an interview with British journalists, General Videla, then the de facto president of Argentina, admitted that lawyers were one of several categories of "subversives" who did not use violence but were nonetheless targets of repression. Christopher Hitchens, "Kissinger Declassified," *Vanity Fair,* December 2004.

3. Jeanne Kirkpatrick, *Dictatorships and Double Standards: Rationalism and Reason in Politics* (New York: Simon & Schuster, 1982).

4. Journalists were also mentioned by Videla in the Hitchens interview (ibid.). There are many journalists among the disappeared. Among the arbitrarily arrested and tortured, then forced into exile, the most prominent was Jacobo Timerman, publisher of an influential daily newspaper, who wrote a memoir of that experience, *Prisoner without a*

Name, Cell without a Number (New York: Vintage, 1988). For more on the systematic submission of the judiciary, see *Nunca Más,* the report of the National Commission on the Disappeared (Argentina's Truth Commission), (New York: Farrar, Straus and Giroux, 1985), as well as a report of a 1979 mission by the Association of the Bar of the City of New York, headed by Orville Schell and Judge Marvin Frankel.

5. Human Rights Watch, "Abu Ghraib Only the 'Tip of the Iceberg,' " Human Rights News, April 27, 2005.

6. The government of President Nestor Kirchner has persuaded Congress to declare the impunity laws null and void, and favors reopening prosecutions, although the matter lies with the judiciary. Decisions declaring the laws unconstitutional were adopted by several district and appellate courts. As of this writing, the leading case is before the Court of Cassation, and it will eventually be decided by the Supreme Court.

7. Comisión Nacional de Verdad y Reconciliación, *Report of the Chilean National Commission on Truth and Reconciliation,* trans. Philip E. Berryman, 2 vols. (Notre Dame, IN: University of Notre Dame Press, 1993). The mandate of the Rettig Commission had included torture only if it had led to the death of the victim.

8. Archdiocese of São Paulo and Joan Dassin, *Torture in Brazil: A Report,* trans. Jaime Wright (New York: Vintage, 1986); Sevicio Paz y Justicia, *Uruguay Nunca Más,* trans. Elizabeth Hampsten (Philadelphia: Temple University Press, 1992). Also, Cynthia Brown and Robert K. Goldman, *Challenging Impunity: The Ley de Caducidad and the Referendum Campaign in Uruguay* (New York: Americas Watch [now Human Rights Watch], 1989), and Lawrence Weschler, *A Miracle, A Universe: Settling Accounts with Torturers* (New York: Pantheon, 1990).

7. *Torture Spoken Here: Ending Global Torture* Minky Worden

1. Jeri Laber, *The Courage of Strangers—Coming of Age with the Human Rights Movement* (New York: PublicAffairs, 2002), p. 230.

2. The U.S. Congressional-Executive Commission was set up by the U.S. Congress in October 2000 with the legislative mandate to monitor human rights and the development of the rule of law in China, and to submit an annual report to the President and the Congress. It is staffed largely by professional China researchers.

3. *U.S. Congressional-Executive Commission 2004 Annual Report.*

4. Scott Long, *In a Time of Torture: The Assault on Justice in Egypt's Crackdown on Homosexual Conduct* (New York: Human Rights Watch, 2004), available at http://hrw.org/reports/2004/egypt0304/.

9. *Sexual Violence, Torture, and International Justice* Cherie Booth

1. See Rory Carroll, "Eight Years of Darkness," *The Guardian,* January 31, 2005.

2. Ibid.

3. See Juliane Kippenberg, "Seeking Justice: The Prosecution of Sexual Violence in the Congo War," Human Rights Watch report, March 2005, available at http://hrw.org/reports/2005/drc0305/; Joanne Csete and Juliane Kippenberg, *War Within the War: Sexual Violence Against Women and Girls in Eastern Congo* (New York: Human Rights Watch, 2002), available at http://hrw.org/reports/2002/drc/.

4. See Timothy L.H. McCormack, "Crimes Against Humanity," in Dominic McGoldrick et al., eds., *The Permanent International Criminal Court: Legal and Policy Issues* (Oxford: Hart Publishing, 2004), p. 196; see also Human Rights Watch Report, 2000, "Federal Republic of Yugoslavia: Kosovo: Rape as a Weapon of 'Ethnic Cleansing,' " Human Rights Watch report, March 2000, available at http://www.hrw.org/reports/2000/fry/.

5. Kanan Makiya, *Cruelty and Silence* (New York: W.W. Norton, 1994), pp. 289–90. To "break someone's eyes" is a Bedouin notion referring to the way Tikriti men in the Ottoman era notoriously destroyed the authority of any non-Tikriti official by ambushing his family and gang-raping his wife in front of him. Similarly, in the 1970s, young women from leading Baghdad families, Sunni and Shi'i, were kidnapped and held captive for several weeks.

6. The Commission for Reception, Truth and Reconciliation in East Timor (CAVR— the Portuguese acronym) is a national, independent, statutory authority. The Commission is mandated to undertake truth-seeking, facilitate community reconciliation, report on its work and findings and make recommendations for further action. For further information, visit the CAVR website at www.easttimor-reconciliation.org.

7. *CAVR UPDATE,* April–May 2003, full report from Public Hearing on Women and Conflict, available at http://www.easttimor-reconciliation.org/cavrUpdate-April May2003-eng.html.

8. See Binaifer Nowrojee, *Shattered Lives: Sexual Violence During the Rwandan Genocide and Its Aftermath* (New York: Human Rights Watch, 1996), available at www.hrw.org/reports/1996/Rwanda.htm.

9. Mary Blewitt, "Remember Rwanda: 10 Years After Genocide," SURF annual review 2003.

10. See Nicholas Kristof, "Bush Puts Ideology over Lives in Sudan," *New York Times,* February 3, 2005.

11. See Theodore Meron, "Rape as a Crime under International Humanitarian Law," 87 *American Journal of International Law* 424 (1993), p. 425, citing Tadeusz Mazowiecki, Special Rapporteur, "Report on the Situation of Human Rights in the Territory of the Former Yugoslavia," A/48/92—S/25341, Annex, pp. 20, 57 (1993).

12. George S. Patton Jr., *War as I Knew It* (Boston: Houghton Mifflin, 1947), p. 23, quoted in Susan Brownmiller, *Against Our Will: Men, Women and Rape* (New York: Simon & Schuster, 1975), p. 23, and cited in Simon Chesterman, "Never Again . . . and Again: Law, Order, and the Gender of War Crimes in Bosnia and Beyond," 22 *Yale Journal of International Law* 299 (1997), p. 324.

13. Chesterman, " "Never Again . . . and Again," p. 328.

14. See Kelly Askin, "Women's Issues in International Criminal Law: Recent Developments and the Potential Contribution of the ICC," in Dinah Shelton, ed., *International Crimes, Peace, and Human Rights: The Role of the International Criminal Court* (Ardsley, NY: Transnational Publishers, 2000), p. 52.

15. See Rhonda Copelon, "Gender Crimes as War Crimes: Integrating Crimes against Women into International Criminal Law," 46 *McGill Law Journal* 217 (2000), pp. 224–25. Copelon points out that rape formed no part of the first series of the ICTR indictments, even though it was included as a crime against humanity in the ICTR Statute and mentioned therein as an example of the war crime of humiliating and degrading treatment. This was notwithstanding the fact that a Human Rights Watch/Federation Internationale des Ligues des Droits de L'Homme report focused on rape and sexual assault in the Taba Commune, over which Jean-Paul Akayesu had control. The same report documented the failure of the prosecutorial staff to take rape seriously, as well as the inappropriateness and lack of training of the investigative staff to undertake rape enquiries.

16. Jan Goodwin, "Rwanda: Justice Denied," *On the Issues* 6, no. 4 (Fall 1997), p. 2, available at http://www.echonyc.com/-onissues/f97rwanda.html.

17. See Askin, "Sexual Violence in Decisions and Indictments of the Yugoslav and Rwandan Tribunals: Current Status," 93 *American Journal of International Law* 97 (1999), pp. 105–6.

18. Under human rights law the pain and suffering caused by rape and sexual assault had for some time already been regarded as constituting torture. See for example the decisions of the European Court of Human Rights in *Aksoy v. Turkey*, 23 *European Human Rights Reports* (1997), paras. 63–64; and *Aydin v. Turkey*, 25 *European Human Rights Reports* (1998), paras. 80–87.

19. Convention against Torture and Other Cruel, Inhuman or Degrading Treatment or Punishment (1984).

20. *Prosecutor v. Jean-Paul Akayesu*, Judgment ICTR-96-4-T of September 2, 1998, para. 687.

21. *Prosecutor v. Zejnil Delalic, Zdravko Mucic, Hazim Delic and Esad Landzo*, Judgment ICTY-96-21-T of November 16, 1998, para. 495.

22. Ibid.

23. Ibid., para. 963. For similar reasons, Delic was also found guilty of torture by rape of the second victim.

24. Ibid.

25. See Kippenberg, "Seeking Justice."

26. See *UN Wire*, "First International Criminal Court Case Targets Uganda's Rebels," January 30, 2004.

27. See Office of the Prosecutor of the International Criminal Court, "Prosecutor Receives Referral of the Situation in the Democratic Republic of the Congo," press release, April 19, 2004.

28. For latest ratification status see www.iccnow.org.

29. In terms of Article 13(b) of the ICC Statute, the UN Security Council is empowered to refer situations to the Court for investigation.

30. *Prosecutor v. Jean-Paul Akayesu*, ICTR, Trial Chamber I, Judgment of September 2, 1998, case no. ICTR-96-4-T, para. 597.

31. ICC Statute Article 7(2)(c).

32. *Kunarac and others*, ICTY Trial Chamber III, Judgment of February 22, 2001, case no. IT-96-23-T, paras. 542–543. Confirmed by the ICTY Appeals Chamber in *Prosecutor v. Kunarac, Kovac and Vukovic*, Judgment, case nos. IT-96-23-A and IT-96-23/1-A, June 12, 2002, at para. 119.

33. See Elements of Crimes, Article 7(1)(f)—Crime Against Humanity of Torture.

34. If a person is to be convicted of torture as a war crime under the ICC Statute, then it will be necessary to prove that the pain inflicted was for the traditional purposes of: obtaining information or a confession, punishment, intimidation or coercion, or for any reason based on discrimination of any kind. See Elements of Crimes, Article 8(2)(a)(II)-1—War Crime of Torture.

35. On cumulation of offenses generally, see Susanne Walther, "Cumulation of Offences," in Antonio Cassese et al., eds., *The Rome Statute of the International Criminal Court: A Commentary—Volume 1* (Oxford: Oxford University Press, 2002), pp. 475–95.

36. See Gerry Simpson, "War Crimes: A Critical Introduction," in Timothy McCormack and Gerry Simpson, eds., *The Law of War Crimes: National and International Approaches* (The Hague: Kluwer Law International, 1997), p. 29.

12. *The Road to Abu Ghraib: Torture and Impunity in U.S. Detention* Reed Brody

1. John Barry, Michael Hirsh, and Michael Isikoff, "The Roots of Terror," *Newsweek,* May 24, 2004.

2. Douglas Jehl and Andrea Elliott, "Cuba Base Sent Its Interrogators to Iraqi Prison," *New York Times,* May 29, 2004.

3. Richard A. Serrano, "Prison Interrogators' Gloves Came Off Before Abu Ghraib," *Los Angeles Times,* June 9, 2004.

4. Human Rights Watch, "The United States' 'Disappeared,' " October 2004, available at http://www.hrw.org/backgrounder/usa/us1004/index.htm.

5. National Commission on Terrorist Attacks upon the United States, *9–11 Commission Report* (New York: W. W. Norton, 2004), p. 379.

6. See Human Rights Watch, "Military Investigations into Treatment of Detainees in U.S. Custody," available at http://www.hrw.org/campaigns/torture/investigations.htm.

7. Even accepting President Bush's incorrect assertion that no Guantánamo detainees were entitled to POW status, the UN Convention against Torture and Other Cruel, Inhuman or Degrading Treatment protects prisoners from the threat of bodily harm to extract information. Indeed, before Abu Ghraib, the U.S. government had condemned the use of dogs on prisoners in other countries.

14. *Command Responsibility for Torture* Dinah Pokempner

1. See Darius Rejali, *Torture and Democracy* (Princeton: Princeton University Press, forthcoming 2005).

2. P.G. Zimbardo, "A Situationalist Perspective on the Psychology of Evil: Understanding How Good People Are Transformed into Perpetrators," in A.G. Miller, ed., *The Social Psychology of Good and Evil* (New York: Guilford Press, 2004), pp. 21–50. See also Susan T. Fiske, Lasana T. Harris, and Amy J.C. Cuddy, "Why Ordinary People Torture Enemy Prisoners," *Science* 306, November 26, 2004.

3. NBC, *Meet the Press,* September 16, 2001, available at http://msnbc.msn.com/id/

3080244/default.htm; also http://www.whitehouse.gov/vicepresident/newsspeeches/speeches/vp20010916.html.

4. Bush's statement at a press appearance with Indonesian President Megawati, available at http://www.whitehouse.gov/news/releases/2001/09/20010919-1html.

5. Douglas Jehl and Andrea Elliott, "Cuba Base Sent Its Interrogators to Iraqi Prison," *New York Times*, May 29, 2004.

6. U.S. Department of Defense, "DoD News Briefing—Secretary Rumsfeld and Gen. Myers," news transcript, January 11, 2002, available at http://www.defenselink.mil/transcripts/2002/t01112002_t0111sd.html.

7. BBC World Edition, "Iraq Abuse Ordered from the Top," June 15, 2004, available at http://news.bbc.co.uk/2/hi/americas/3806713.stm.

8. President George W. Bush, Secretary of State Colin Powell, and Attorney General John Ashcroft, "President Urges Readiness and Patience," September 15, 2001, available at http://www.whitehouse.gov/news/releases/2001/09/20010915-4.html; President George W. Bush, "Guard and Reserves 'Define Spirit of America,' " September 17, 2001, available at http://www.whitehouse.gov/news/releases/2001/09/20010917-3.html. These sorts of words seem to have inspired a man threatening to bomb villagers in Tora Bora if they didn't turn over Arabs, a law review essay considering state responsibility for war crimes inspired by such cowboy talk, and perhaps a defense strategy for a CIA interrogator charged with assaulting an Afghani. See Dayna L. Kaufman, "Note, Don't Do What I Say, Do What I Mean! Assessing a State's Responsibility for the Exploits of Individuals Acting in Conformity with a Statement from a Head of State," 70 *Fordham Law Review* 2603 (May 2002); and "Interrogator's Defenders Cite Bush," *International Herald Tribune Online*, February 12, 2005, available at http://www.iht.com/articles/2005/02/11/news/defense.html.

9. Cofer Black was the director of the CIA's Counterterrorist Center from 1999 to 2002. See testimony, September 26, 2002, Joint House and Senate Intelligence Committees.

10. Mark Danner, "Abu Ghraib: The Hidden Story," *New York Review of Books*, October 7, 2004, available at http://www.markdanner.com/nyreview/100704_print.htm.

11. Josh White, "Soldiers' 'Wish Lists' of Detainee Tactics Cited," *Washington Post*, April 19, 2005, p. A16, available at http://www.washingtonpost.com/wp-dyn/articles/A64409-2005Apr18.html.

12. Convention against Torture and Other Forms of Cruel, Inhuman or Degrading Treatment, Article 2.2. Article 16.2 of the same convention provides that the convention is without prejudice to other international and domestic instruments regulating cruel, in-

human, and degrading treatment. The prohibition of such treatment is nonderogable under the International Covenant on Civil and Political Rights, to which the United States and 153 other nations are parties. It is important to keep in mind how settled the law is on the absolute quality of the ban to appreciate how radical a departure the academic proponents of "regulatory torture" are making.

13. Yuval Ginbar, "Back to a Routine of Torture: Torture and Ill-Treatment of Palestinian Detainees during Arrest Detention and Interrogation," Public Committee Against Torture in Israel, September 2001–April 2003, available at http://www.stoptorture.org.il/eng/images/uploaded/publications/58.pdf.

14. Daniel Muñoz-Rojas and Jean-Jacques Frésard, "The Roots of Behaviour in War: Understanding and Preventing IHL Violations," *International Review of the Red Cross* 853, March 31, 2004, pp. 189–206.

15. Diederick Lohman, "The Wrongs of Passage: Inhuman and Degrading Treatment of Recruits in the Russian Army," Human Rights Watch report, October 2004.

16. No one in the administration has made the claim so far that they in fact knowingly authorized unlawful and unethical treatment under a moral compulsion to protect the greater social interest—a classic formulation of the clash between utilitarian and absolutist ethics in the performance of public duty. See Michael Walzer, "Political Action: The Problem of Dirty Hands," *Philosophy and Public Affairs* 2, no. 2 (1973). Walzer, in discussing Weber's vision of a "suffering" public servant, writes: "But sometimes the hero's suffering needs to be socially expressed (for like punishment, it confirms and reinforces our sense that certain acts are wrong). And equally important, it sometimes needs to be socially limited. We don't want to be ruled by men who have lost their souls." Ibid., p. 177.

17. This is known as the "problem of many hands." While a pure Kantian view may hold a person responsible only for what she intends, we more typically hold someone also responsible for what she knows will be the probable consequences of her act. See Dennis F. Thompson, "Moral Responsibility of Public Officials: The Problem of Many Hands," *American Political Science Review* 74, no. 4 (1980), p. 912.

18. Scott Horton, interview with Gwen Ifil on the PBS *NewsHour with Jim Lehrer*, August 25, 2004, transcript available at http://www.pbs.org/newshour/bb/military/july-dec04/abughraib_8-25.html.

19. John Yoo argues that the Abu Ghraib abuses "had nothing to do" with the OLC memoranda he helped draft on torture and the applicability of the Geneva Conventions, though the question, of course, is whether the memoranda had something to do with

the abuses. Tom Ridge, the outgoing chief of the Department of Homeland Security, said that under extreme circumstances, such as the threat of a terrorist nuclear attack, it would be "human nature" to torture "to extract information." BBC News, "US 'Should Not Rule Out Torture,' " January 15, 2005, available at http://news .bbc.co.uk/2/hi/americas/4175713.stm. Heather MacDonald disparages the "torture narrative" and the idea that sleep deprivation or prolonged forced stress positions could amount to torture, and argues that it is important to upset the expectations of terrorists that the United States is "weak" because it is unwilling to torture.

20. Jeremy Waldron, in a forthcoming article in the *Columbia Law Review,* argues that the norm against torture is a legal archetype in our normative system, that is, a norm of heightened significance in that it epitomizes an underlying principle of our legal system: to wit, that law is no longer connected to brutality. Among the areas of law he identifies that could be threatened by revision of the norm are the constitutional prohibition of cruel and unusual punishment and the notions of substantive and procedural due process; indeed, it is so embedded in our notion of the rule of law itself that the damage to it threatens more generally our respect for such systems as the Geneva Conventions, human rights law, and the separation of emergency or wartime rules from rule of law in peacetime. See Waldron, "Torture and Positive Law: Jurisprudence for the White House," public lecture, Victoria University of Wellington, New Zealand, August 19, 2004; revised version for Boalt Hall GALA Workshop, September 30, 2004.

15. *Torture in U.S. Prisons* Jamie Fellner

1. "Implications of Abu Ghraib for the American Prison System," speech delivered at the Vera Institute of Justice, June 22, 2004.

16. *Justifying Torture* Kenneth Roth

1. Human Rights Watch, "Malaysia: PM's Visit Puts Spotlight on Detainee Abuse," July 19, 2004.

2. BBC News, " 'Torture Intelligence' Criticised," October 11, 2004, available at http://news.bbc.co.uk/1/hi/uk/3732488.stm.

3. Douglas Jehl, "C.I.A. Is Seen as Seeking New Role on Detainees," *New York Times,* February 16, 2005.

4. *Wall Street Journal,* "Red Double-Crossed Again," editorial, December 2, 2004.

5. Testimony of Cofer Black, former director of the CIA's Counterterrorism Center, before a joint session of the Senate and the House Intelligence Committees, September 26, 2002.

6. Douglas Jehl, "Questions Are Left by C.I.A. Chief on the Use of Torture," *New York Times,* March 18, 2005.

7. Dana Priest, "CIA's Assurances on Transferred Suspects Doubted," *Washington Post,* March 17, 2005.

8. Neil A. Lewis, "Red Cross Finds Detainee Abuse in Guantánamo," *New York Times,* November 30, 2004.

9. Memorandum to the President from Alberto R. Gonzales, January 25, 2005.